KU-488-223

THE MODERN MOVEMENT

ONE HUNDRED KEY BOOKS

FROM ENGLAND, FRANCE AND AMERICA

1880-1950

By the same author

THE ROCK POOL
ENEMIES OF PROMISE
THE UNQUIET GRAVE
THE CONDEMNED PLAYGROUND
THE MISSING DIPLOMATS
IDEAS AND PLACES
PREVIOUS CONVICTIONS

LES PAVILLONS
(*co-author*)

THE MODERN MOVEMENT

ONE HUNDRED KEY BOOKS

FROM ENGLAND, FRANCE AND AMERICA

1880-1950

CHOSEN BY

CYRIL CONNOLLY

BIBLIOGRAPHY OF ENGLISH AND FRENCH EDITIONS

G. D. E. SOAR

B.A., A.L.A.

A GRAFTON BOOK

ANDRE DEUTSCH

HAMISH HAMILTON

First published in Great Britain, 1965
jointly by André Deutsch Ltd, and
Hamish Hamilton Ltd London

Printed in Great Britain by
T. & A. Constable Ltd, Hopetoun Street, Edinburgh
Printers to the University of Edinburgh

TO

MAURICE BOWRA

CONTENTS

THE MODERN MOVEMENT

page 1

PART ONE

1880-1920

page 13

PART TWO

1920-1930

page 45

PART THREE

1930-1940

page 67

PART FOUR

1940-1950

page 85

BIBLIOGRAPHY

page 97

THE MODERN MOVEMENT

THE Modern Movement began as a revolt against the bourgeois in France, the Victorians in England, the puritanism and materialism of America. The modern spirit was a combination of certain intellectual qualities inherited from the Enlightenment: lucidity, irony, scepticism, intellectual curiosity, combined with the passionate intensity and enhanced sensibility of the Romantics, their rebellion and sense of technical experiment, their awareness of living in a tragic age. The crucial generation, the generation which reconciled these opposites, was that of Baudelaire, Flaubert, and Dostoievsky (born in 1821), of Whitman, Melville and Ruskin (b. 1819), of Edmond de Goncourt and Matthew Arnold (1822), to which one might add Renan (1823), Turgenev (1818), and Courbet (1819), to complete the picture. All these artists, we feel, have something which reaches out to our own age although so much of them belongs to the past, all are difficult to pin down, to analyse, to put into categories, because of the duality in their own natures resulting from their inheritance of critical intelligence and exploring sensibility.

One sees this inheritance stemming from Voltaire and d'Holbach on the one side, Rousseau and Diderot on the other, with Stendhal and Constant, Chateaubriand and Chenier widening the breach—(Daudet called Flaubert '*le confluent de Chateaubriand avec Balzac*')—but in this welter of precursors one cannot at any time point and say: 'This is the Modern Movement.' Flaubert died in 1880, the year in which Apollinaire was born, only a year or two before Pound, Picasso, and E. M. Forster who are still alive saw the light and six years after Somerset Maugham. 1880 seems to me the point at which the Modern Movement can be diagnosed as an event which is still modern to us, more modern than many of us, not something put away in the moth-balls of history. So I have taken it as a point of departure though both Baudelaire and Flaubert reach into it through the power of their posthumous works, the Letters which, in Flaubert's case, constituted the bible of Art for Art's Sake, his explosive anti-bourgeois satire, *Bouvard et Pécuchet* (1881), and Baudelaire's two devastating journals which were not published till 1887.

Flaubert and Baudelaire: our two fallen fathers, ruined, destroyed, tragic yet each a beacon light glowing for posterity, Baudelaire's fitfully from his mother's home at Honfleur, Flaubert's unbrokenly from his house at Croisset, illuminating the two banks of the Seine, the waterway to Paris, Trouville, Deauville, Honfleur, Rouen . . . (Flaubert's grandmother's family was called Cambremer!). The Miss Colliers whom he adored on the beach, his '*fantômes de Trouville*', were the original '*jeunes filles en fleurs*' though, like Baudelaire, he preferred exotic women.

Born in the same year, with six letters of their names in common, achieving fame within a year (1856-7) with two masterpieces, *Madame Bovary* and *Les Fleurs du Mal*, both of which were prosecuted, Flaubert with a mother who would never let go of him, Baudelaire with a mother of whom he would never let go ('You have no right to re-marry with a son like me'), they would seem to entangle and yet they probably met only once or twice at Madame Sabatier's.

After the novelist had praised *Les Fleurs du Mal*—'*Ah, vous comprenez l'embêtement de l'existence, vous! Vous pouvez vous vanter de cela sans orgueil*'—Baudelaire invited Flaubert to his mother's at Honfleur, but nothing came of it.

In 1858 the Goncourts coined the word 'Modernity'* while Gautier, to whom *Les Fleurs du Mal* was dedicated and who also adored Flaubert, '*un grand génie, tous ses livres des chefs d'oeuvre*', contributed out of his lifetime of glorious hackery the celebrated phrase which belongs to the Movement, '*Toute ma valeur . . . c'est que je suis un homme pour qui le monde visible existe.*'

Although Flaubert influenced many writers of the golden age of the Modern Movement, particularly Conrad (who began *Nostromo* on the end papers of his *Éducation sentimentale*), Joyce and Pound, he was accepted only with reservations by Proust and Valéry and has not exercised the magic of Baudelaire on succeeding generations. There is a starkness about the poet's intelligence as in the phrase he used to his mother to describe his love affair with the half-caste Jeanne Duval:

'*Cela a duré assez longtemps mais enfin c'est fini*',

which might have been his comment on his own life. After being for many years the private literary property of Arthur Symons he has emerged to be re-interpreted by Sartre and magnificently translated by Robert Lowell.

Only when we drink poison are we well—
We want, this fire so burns our brain tissue,
To drown in the abyss—heaven or hell,
Who cares? Through the unknown, we'll find the *new*.

The 'seventies were the decade of Verlaine and Zola, of the beginnings of Henry James and Tolstoy, of Meredith and Swinburne, of Poe's influence and of Rimbaud's fugue with Verlaine. A generation of truly modern writers emerges, all highly sophisticated, and all owing something to Flaubert

* But Littré cites Gautier for the word a few years later.

and Baudelaire—James (b. 1843), Mallarmé (1842), Villiers de l'Isle—Adam (1838), Verlaine (1844), Huysmans (1848), and the mysterious Lautréamont (1846).

Villiers' talent petered out; he talked and drank it away, but his gifts were prodigious. 'Everything that's mine I owe to him' (Maeterlinck). Claudel, writing to Gide, recalls how in his young days he used to see Verlaine and Villiers 'with want in their eyes, wearing the remains of their talent like a moth-eaten old fur-piece round their necks'. Rimbaud aside, Mallarmé and Huysmans almost created the modern sensibility between them, while both Yeats and Valéry attended on the schoolmaster-poet who had discovered that the only universe he could bear to inhabit must proceed from his own head. Writing to Debussy about his setting of the *Après-midi d'un Faune* Mallarmé said: 'Your illustration conforms exactly to my text except that it goes even further *dans la nostalgie et la lumière, avec finesse, avec malaise, avec richesse.*' Is not this what we mean by modern sensibility? It could never have been written before.

With the generation of Debussy (b. 1862), Yeats (1865), Gide (1869), Proust and Valéry (1871), Jarry (1873) we come within living memory and it is a short step to the generation of the 1880's, to Eliot, Pound, Lawrence and Joyce, to Virginia Woolf and Edith Sitwell and Marianne Moore, and from them to Hemingway, Cummings, Faulkner, Malraux, Huxley, Graves, and so to Auden and our own day. The French fathered the Modern Movement, which slowly moved beyond the Channel and then across the Irish Sea until the Americans finally took it over, bringing to it their own demonic energy, extremism and taste for the colossal.

As we look back across the drifting formlessness of contemporary literature, we see that the Movement had a shape —and that the peak period was from about 1910 to 1925, a period of creativity which included the Eliot of 'Prufrock', 'The Waste Land' and 'The Hollow Men', the Pound of the lyrics and early cantos, the later Yeats, the heyday of Virginia Woolf and Lytton Strachey, the Joyce of *The Portrait*, *Ulysses* and the first *Anna Livia*, the poetry of Apollinaire and Valéry, the novel of Proust, the emergence of Hemingway, Cummings, Lewis, Wallace Stevens, W. C. Williams, Forster's *Passage to India*, Fitzgerald's *The Great Gatsby*, the preaching of Lawrence, the giggle of Firbank, the candour of Gide. It was also the great age of Cubism, and the beginnings of Surrealism, of Ravel and Stravinsky and Cocteau and the Russian Ballet. The Great War cut across the Movement, deflecting it but unable to stem its vitality. The late 'twenties show a falling off but the angry 'thirties introduce the political themes which sent many writers back to realism. At the end of the 'thirties works like *Finnegans Wake* or Gide's *Journal* or *Between The Acts* resound like farewells and epitaphs. Yeats (b. 1865), Joyce, Virginia Woolf (both b. 1882) are gone within six months of each other and everything the Movement stood for is dubbed 'degenerate art'—or converted to propaganda. The Titans depart, the theses begin.

As all objectives were gained and the complacent hypocrisy of the nineteenth century punctured, its materialism exposed, the Movement ground to a halt; technical innovations were by-passed, originality incorporated into the norm, until rebellion grew meaningless, though it may yet persist in authoritarian countries or where censorship and intolerance dominate as with unrevised attitudes to drug-addiction or homosexuality (Burroughs and the Beats)—and gone too the corresponding movements in the Arts—Post-Impressionism, Fauvism, Cubism, Surrealism, Abstract Expressionism—with their ramifications in many countries. It has nevertheless dominated the life-time of the over-forties, some of whom have never recovered from their youthful intoxication, and its survivors—Picasso, Stravinsky, Pound and Forster whose art, like Yeats' and Eliot's could wind the marrow from our bones—remain our grand old men.

In preparing this list I have tried to choose books with outstanding originality and richness of texture and with the spark of rebellion alight, books which aspire to be works of art. Realism is not enough. There is nothing specifically modern about realism and too often it goes with undigested documentary and unimaginative technique. Zola may be an exception but his full impact was made before the period. The other objections, however, apply to Dreiser, Wells, Bennett, Galsworthy, Lewis, Dos Passos, Farrell and many chain novels about a family. For similar reasons traditionalists are excluded and this means many Catholic writers. If we apply the awareness of Rimbaud, Baudelaire, Flaubert as a touchstone we must exclude as traditionalist not only Chesterton, Belloc, Kipling, Hardy (as a novelist) but Housman, De la Mare, even Robert Frost (Georgian-Wordsworthian-New England) and most of the poetry of Robert Graves. This is an important point since novelists, on the whole, are not avant-garde and depend solidly on tradition, even when their outlook is affected by the Modern Movement (David Garnett, Osbert Sitwell, Elizabeth Bowen, Anthony Powell, Carson McCullers). The new avant-garde novel or anti-novel (Beckett, Butor, Robbe-Grillet) falls just outside my date-line.

But awareness is not in itself sufficient. Arthur Symons, for example, was steeped in the Modern Movement, haunted by Baudelaire, the interpreter of symbolism for Yeats and Eliot and a prolific poet in his own right but he simply was not the book of collected poems in which they first appeared. Thus Eliot's 'Prufrock' and 'The Waste Land' (30*a* and *b*), count as one book, *Poems 1909-25*. These are the only liberties I have taken. For every book that I should like to put in, there is one that will have to come out. That, in a selection bridging seventy years, is where the squeeze is felt.

good enough. Genius was lacking, scholarship hazy, taste and talent spread too thin. Aldington was such another. Wilde imitated Flaubert in *Salome* and Huysmans in *Dorian Gray* but his true gift (apart from conversation) lay in traditional Congrevian comedy. Synge, however, soaked like Wilde and Symons in the Symbolists, produced a revolutionary masterpiece. (This is nearly true of *The Ballad of Reading Gaol* which mounts a streamlined offensive on capital punishment and prison conditions but in the most hackneyed Ancient Mariner stanza, complete with archaisms.) It would be to fall into just the fault which we deplore in realism to include certain books because they are the first to defend abortion or explain relativity.

Furthermore, I have limited my list to French, English and American literature because, without knowing German or Russian, I cannot absolutely judge a book from a translation, however perfect, and because the dates at which translations appear confuse the time-scale. This means the exclusion of Tolstoy, Dostoievsky, Turgenev and Tchekov, of *Oblomov* and Bunin's *Gentleman from San Francisco*, of Rilke, Mann (alas for *Death in Venice*), of Kafka, Musil, Kavafy, Ungaretti and Svevo, of Lorca and Pasternak; to include these writers would also enormously lengthen the list and I can only say that one hundred books is enough and that the three literatures I have chosen have always been in close communication.

I have also excluded translations except Waley's *Translations from the Chinese* which can surely be judged as an original contribution to our poetry, and Koestler's *Darkness at Noon* as it was first published in this country. I have assumed that we can all read French in the original but have also given the most recent translations of all French books mentioned. (Valéry's *La Jeune Parque* has only just been translated.)

Many good, even great books are not key books; they come too late in the day when the author is already well known and has made his mark on the Movement or they repeat an early success or explore a backwater. This problem is extremely difficult with Henry James or George Moore, for example, whose brightest novel, *Esther Waters*, is also one of his most derivative. Conrad poses a similar problem. And there are books which are marred by auto-intoxicated rhetoric like those of Thomas Wolfe (a plaster colossus) and the monologrolling of Henry Miller. Some 'key' writers do not, in my opinion, produce a key book. Verlaine is one of these unless we accept *Sagesse* (1881). Music is not enough either. This also applies to Laforgue whose poems, I feel, despite their influence on Eliot, are really very slender and whose *Moralités légendaires* are forced and whimsical. He died too young and so did Dowson whom I must fail to include for similar reasons.

The worst headache has been over writers whom I think ought to be in but whom I do not enjoy enough to feel prepared to take away with me into solitary confinement. Hypocrisy would certainly be found out so I hereby declare these blind spots: Claudel, Max Jacob, St John Perse, Roussel (whose mechanistic anti-humanism is now coming into vogue), Faulkner (though I have chosen his easiest book), Eluard whose poetry never seems to me to come to the boil (except in one or two war-time lyrics), Gertrude Stein, since I cannot stomach the torrent of her automatic writing nor the greedy show-biz of the autobiographies—and well-camouflaged anti-modernists like Max Beerbohm and the Baron Corvo.

The list is literary and one-culture, and must exclude scientific, historical and philosophical works because of difficulties of evaluation. The very thought of placing Bergson,

G. E. Moore, Bradley, William James, Frazer, Fre
Spengler, Pareto, Bertrand Russell, Santayana, Wittgens
and A. J. Ayer makes the anthologist shudder. Where is
frontier between science and literature? There is no sp
to indulge one's eccentricity. Works of reference are a
excluded (Fowler), together with theories of literary critici
(Richards, Empson), books on art and by artists, antholog
and almost all criticism and biography. I have admitt
three books of criticism: Wilson's *Axel's Castle*, Elio
Selected Essays, and James's *Prefaces*. The only biography
Eminent Victorians—the only autobiographies are Gid
and Robert Graves'. (Henry Adams does not write w
enough.) Most autobiographies fail as works of art throu
ancestor-worship or the inclusion of secondary material.

The last part of my list proved more treacherous than th
beginning. While I feel 1880-1950 is right, the 'forties a
still painfully close. I made my selection here from som
sixty books, trying to weigh *Between the Acts* beside *New Ye
Letter*, *Lord Weary's Castle* against *Under the Volcano*. When i
doubt prefer genius, but how to be sure of it? ' "*Mon Dieu
mon Dieu!*" *soupira des Esseintes* "*qu'il existe donc peu de livre
qu'on puisse relire*".' In a period where literary taste is changin
so rapidly much may already appear incomprehensible. On
seems to be sticking paper-flags into a dissolving sand-castle
while in full erosion oneself. Try as we would to be objective
any such list (exhibition of compulsive pedantry or debt o
gratitude?) is personal as a cardiogram. It may well prov
the last unsponsored by a faculty.

A word on the numbering. Chain novels are treated as one
(example: Proust). Very scarce but significant slim volume
are mentioned separately with an '*a*' or '*b*' but numbered by

PART I

1880-1920

1880-1920

THE HEROIC ERA

1880-1900

THE period of French domination, when half a dozen masterpieces established a new sensibility (already apparent in some of Baudelaire's poems and many of his poems in prose). Some of these seminal works were first published in the 'eighties and disseminated by Verlaine's *Les Poètes maudits* (1884) or Arthur Symons' *Symbolist Movement in Literature* (1899) or Moore's *Confessions of a Young Man* (1888): Swinburne, Meredith, Melville, Whitman are among Anglo-Saxon precursors. I consider the 'nineties a dead end, essentially the English version of Symbolism, for, if we subtract the *fin de siècle* element, there is very little left. Mark Twain's *Huckleberry Finn* (1884) I think is over-praised, too involved and sentimental despite its prophetic use of American vernacular—a false dawn—and, therefore, although it has won the admiration of Eliot, Hemingway and Trilling, excluded.

The intellectual climate of the period can best be savoured in Huysmans' account of Des Esseintes' library in *A Rebours* (1884) particularly in its modern section which is uncannily prescient of our taste today. After citing Petronius, Apuleius, Villon, Pascal, he comes down heavily for Baudelaire. 'His admiration for that writer was boundless' and he gives a three-page analysis of the poet's '*insondable tristesse*' his disillusion and his style 'which above all others had the magical ability to pin down with a peculiar vitality of phrase the most fugitive and elusive psychological states, moments of morbid melancholy and exhaustion'; he particularly admired the *Mort des Amants* and the prose poem '*Anywhere out of this World*', '*L'Ennemi*' and his translation of Poe's '*Adventures of Arthur Gordon Pym*'. He also admired Flaubert's *Tentation*, Barbey's *Diaboliques*, Goncourt's *Faustin*, Zola's *L'Assommoir*, and—among his contemporaries—Verlaine (particularly the poems '*Streets*' or '*Dansons la Gigue*' with its curious metre which was to be re-immortalised by Debussy), Tristan Corbière, eccentric author of *Les Amours jaunes* (1873), and above all Villiers and Mallarmé. He greatly appreciated the delicately supernatural tales of Villiers, the '*Intersigne*' and '*Véra*' which he thought a small masterpiece '*Ici l'hallucination était empreinte d'une tendresse exquise*' (as in James's *Altar of the Dead*).

He praises four of the *Contes Cruels* for their ferocious wit and black humour, their savage denigration of the bourgeois epoch. He also enjoyed Charles Cros—but, beyond all, Mallarmé of whom, as with Baudelaire, he had had printed his own selection on special papers—*L'Azur*, *Hérodiade*, *Les Fenêtres*, *L'Après-midi d'un Faune*, each, of course, in highly significant bindings. No wonder his creator Huysmans was told in a review by Barbey that he must decide between the muzzle of a revolver and the foot of the cross! Ten years later, he had chosen—as several later revolutionaries in the Movement were to choose.

One can only wish that Des Esseintes had discovered Rimbaud and had also included an English section. He must, given the anglophilia which got him as far as the Taverne Anglaise in the Rue d'Amsterdam, have read Dickens as well as Poe—why not *Modern Love*, or Pater's *Renaissance*? One detects a reciprocal blankness between James and Huysmans.

Yet the 'eighties and 'nineties are overshadowed by James whose work culminates at the end of the century in the brilliant series of novels and stories—the *Spoils of Poynton* and *What Maisie Knew*, *The Awkward Age* and *The Sacred Fount* and the series of tales dealing with the frustrations of the literary life, *Terminations*, *Embarrassments*, *The Two Magics*. To include more than one of these would capsize this little craft before it had left port. Where James, whose work moreover does not completely belong to the Movement, is concerned, I consider I have been able to make but a token selection.

-1 HENRY JAMES (1843-1916)
PORTRAIT OF A LADY (1881)

(Re-issued as a Penguin 1963)

Written in James' earlier manner (serialised through 1880) on James' favourite theme, the involvement of American youth and innocence (Isabel Archer) in European guile; 'a great leisurely built cathedral' (Graham Greene). 'The waterside life, the wondrous lagoon spread before me and the ceaseless human chatter of Venice came in at my windows, to which I seem to myself to have been constantly driven in the furious fidget of composition'.

Although Hawthorne had written of Americans in Europe, James brought them into the field of literature, they became his special subject, his *donnée*. It was through him that the world of the American expatriates first found its voice; that Europe learnt to respect the contribution which they brought to it. He gave them their myth. Daisy Miller, uncomprehended and misjudged by Roman society of the 'seventies, makes way for Edith Wharton, Mrs Chanler and other Jamesians who conquered it a generation later. The *Portrait* supplies a key theme to be revised by the Americans of the 'twenties, the expatriate Bohemians.

2 GUSTAVE FLAUBERT (1821-1880)
BOUVARD ET PÉCUCHET

(1880, posthumous)

With preface by Maupassant 1881, translated 1936 by G. W. Stonier and T. W. Earp (Cape and New Directions), the ending reconstituted by Raymond Queneau, with an important introduction, Paris, 1946. Overwork on this encyclopedia of human ignorance contributed to Flaubert's death. (He read more than 1,500 books for it.) His two clerks, one fat, one thin, set out to explore all knowledge and analyse every branch of study, always enthusiastic, always meeting with increasing hostility and confusion. Polymath pessimism is irradiated by gleams of poetry: slapstick fused with the sadness of things: understandably Joyce's favourite book. Their legacy spent, their reputations damaged, their health ruined and their curiosity drained by bootless speculation, the two clerks return to copying again, a procession of conflicting theories and addled emotions their only reward. 'Bouvard' was followed through the 'eighties by the publication of the five volumes of Flaubert's letters, preaching the religion of art as the supreme justification of existence, a post-symbolist bible whose music still haunts us like the baying of a lost hound.

3 VILLIERS DE L'ISLE—ADAM (1838-1889)
CONTES CRUELS (1883)

Translated *Cruel Tales* by Robert Baldick (O.U.P., 1963). This master-storyteller combines a high romantic sensibility with a devastating anti-bourgeois irony. 'Living? Our servants will do it for us.' His *L'Eve Future* was a forerunner of science-fiction, his drama *Axel* with its symbolic renunciations gave Edmund Wilson his point of departure and deeply influenced Yeats. Villiers died in want, talking away his plots to greedy eavesdroppers. Mallarmé delivered a famous lecture on him (1890) beginning '*un homme au rêve habitué, vient ici parler d'un autre, qui est mort*'. He and Huysmans were the last to stay with him at his death and fulfil his wishes—and indeed, impose their own—for the dying poet was made to marry his old mistress in order to legitimise his child. The ceremony revealed that she could not sign her name, a final humiliation for him, but it gave her the right to remain with him in the hospital through the nights and thus save him from dying alone. Verlaine also had a deep admiration for him and made him one of his *poètes maudits* because '*il n'est pas assez glorieux en ces temps qui devraient être à ses pieds*' . . . How much more true today!

-4 JORIS KARL HUYSMANS (1848-1907)
À REBOURS (1884)

Translated as *Against the Grain*. Des Esseintes, the aristocratic robot who lived for the rarefication of his sensibility was intended as a study in pride and neurosis, but found himself 'the Breviary of the Decadents' instead. Comte Robert de Montesquiou, the dilettante original, later served as part model for Proust's Charlus. His selfish aestheticism and abandonment to sensual wear and tear does not exclude some excellent appreciations of Baudelaire, Villiers, Mallarmé and Gustave Moreau (then little known). *Dorian Gray* bound several copies to suit mood and season, and the young Valéry read it five times—'*Ne me méprisez pas trop, mais il est mon livre....*' 'When I am tired of contemplating my own personality, I sample the pages on Moreau's *Salome* or the imaginary journey to London, or the curiously flat ending and I rejoice in my heart.' '*Le Roman ainsi conçu ainsi condensé en une page ou deux deviendrait une communion de pensée entre un magique écrivain et un idéal lecteur*' (Des Esseintes).

5 CHARLES BAUDELAIRE (1821-1867)
OEUVRES POSTHUMES (1887)

Contains, besides some of his finest letters, his life by the editor, E. Crépet, and the two diaries, '*Mon Coeur mis à nu*' and '*Fusées*' (translated by C. Isherwood with preface by Eliot, 1934, with later preface by Auden [N.Y.], best editions Sartre, Paris, 1946, and J. Crépet and Blin, Paris, Corti, 1949). The 'journals' are tragic, ineluctable, obsessive; composed in his last years, just before he went mad. 'I have cultivated my hysteria with delight and terror. Now I suffer continually from vertigo, and today, 23rd January 1862, I have received a singular warning. I have felt the wind of the wing of madness pass over me' (tr. Isherwood). Beneath the tense, abrupt, incisive prose, best of its kind since Pascal, one is aware of a pathetic weakness of will, a mind made lucid by approaching doom, through which remorse flashes like lightning. '*Vous êtes résistant comme le marbre et pénétrant comme un brouillard d'Angleterre*' (Flaubert).

6 ARTHUR RIMBAUD (1854-1891)
LES ILLUMINATIONS (1886)

(Translated by Helen Rootham)

'Il faut être absolument moderne . . .'

Reprinted with '*Une Saison en enfer*', 1892. Born in 1854 Rimbaud gave up writing by the time he was twenty; it took many years for Verlaine's prefaces and the sketch in *Les Poètes Maudits* to establish his reputation which has since dominated modern literature, chiefly through these mysteriously exciting prose poems (some written in England), which wed an hallucinated inspiration to a classical purity of form. '*Toujours épaté. Vraiment ce bougre-là a deviné et crée la littérature qui reste toujours au-dessus du lecteur*' (Valéry to Gide). 'A mystic in the primitive phase' (Claudel). Verlaine's description of this supreme adolescent in his *Poètes maudits* is unforgettable. '*L'homme était grand, bien bâti, prèsque athlétique, visage parfaitement ovale d'ange en exil, avec des cheveux châtain-clair mal en ordre et des yeux d'un bleu pâle inquiétant.*'

7 STÉPHANE MALLARMÉ (1842-1898)
POESIES (1887)

The poems translated by Roger Fry, and the '*Après-midi d'un Faune*' by Aldous Huxley. Reprinted often with additions. Another advance in sensibility, perhaps the most rarefied in western literature, especially in his diaphanously ethereal sonnets. This grand-master of the Symbolists, friend of Huysmans and protector of Villiers, was an inspirer of Yeats, Moore, Georg and Valéry. '*Notre Mallarmé—Mallarmé, événement de nos jeunesses. Mallarmé, toujours présent et presque* *toujours sensible et reconnaissable dans les esprits, dans les jugements de tous ceux qui l'ont approché, vénére, distingué à jamais de tous les hommes qu'ils ont pu voir'* . . . (Valéry, Letters).*

- 8 GUY DE MAUPASSANT (1850-1893)
BEL AMI (1885)

Translated by Eric Sutton (Hamish Hamilton, 1948). Born in 1850, Maupassant died insane from syphilis in 1893. 'Another man for the scrap-heap' he cried to his valet after trying to kill himself. In his brief life, largely devoted to his master Flaubert (who may possibly have been his father as well as his fellow Norman and family friend), he arrived almost effortlessly at a perfectly simple, direct and ageless style and at a comprehension of the lower nature of men and women and their secret motivations which amounted to genius. The women he understood so well literally mobbed him to death. *Bel Ami* is his most successful novel, for his art was usually expended on the short story of which he was the master (*Boule de Suif*, *La Maison Tellier*). Duroy is indeed a hero of our time, and though intended as the portrait of a cad, he seems now a perfectly normal modern careerist, a cake-eater climbing to the top through journalism and politics with as weapons sex appeal, lack of scruple and a cynical resentment against the rich. *Bel Ami* appealed to his creator who named the yacht where he spent his last happy days (*Sur l'eau*) after him. Patron saint of best sellers, he has profoundly influenced Maugham, Bennett and many others. Only a master could so economically describe the opening

* During the Occupation a French Doctor, Henri Mondor (author of works on cancer of the rectum and gonorrheal arthritis) devoted several years to a monumental biography of Mallarmé which traces this most sedentary of authors through every nuance of his artistic development.

scene on the Boulevards, the rendezvous in the church of La Trinité, the Duel, or the final hypocrisy of the Grand Wedding. Some of the gifts which Flaubert worked so hard to acquire were his by nature; he took duck-wise to the water despite his mentor's anxious recriminations, and drowned in it.

9 EDMOND (1822-1896) AND JULES (1830-1870) DE GONCOURT

JOURNAL

(Published from 1887-96)

English Selection from the unabridged Journal by Robert Baldick (Oxford, 1962). Jules collaborated on the first three volumes; the total was nine. The journal (opening with 1851) gives a sophisticated modern account of one of the most engrossing periods of literary history: Paris a century ago. Though extremely jealous of talent in others, both were excellent observers and there has been no one quite like them before or since. They were backward-looking aristocratic aesthetes like Des Esseintes yet realistic novelists at the same time. Full-length portraits and recorded conversations of Flaubert, Turgenev, Daudet, Zola, Taine, Renan, who attended the 'Dinners at Magny's' (falling off in zest after 1880). 'They believed everything' (Daudet). 'Journal full of lies' (Claretie). Edmond '*présomptueux*', Jules, *faussement gavroche, très snob*'. Baudelaire thought them conceited and Flaubert reproached them. No *praise* in the Journals—everyone is cut down by them to size—their size. Pre-occupation, for the first time, with writer's sex-lives and their ailments, especially of digestion and the bladder. Much envy, especially of Flaubert and Zola, disguised as commiseration. Typical comment, on

Maupassant (in the train to Flaubert's funeral), 'one can see from his brick-red complexion that *he* won't make old bones.'

10 J. K. HUYSMANS (1848-1907)
LÀ-BAS (1891)

Translated as *Down There*. This, his greatest novel, is marvellously constructed. The fugue between the life of Gilles de Retz (announced by the digression on Grünewald's crucifixion) and the satanic experiments with Madame H. is so worked out that the evil element increases in each, the Black Mass looming over the present even as the orgies at Tiffauges dominate the mediaeval past until the clouds move away after the rupture with Madame H., the healing of the astrologer, the repentance of de Retz—the whole sombre adventure of the imagination painted against the dull grey background of Saint-Sulpice and Durtal's book-lined apartment. The last book before his conversion and based on his own experience —a descending spiral of anxiety—before the crucial visit to the Abbé Mugnier. It opens with an attack on the inadequacy of realism and the Zola school. Surrealists prefer *En Rade* ('87) on account of some vitriolic sequences by this Swiftian expert on discomfort.

11 ALFRED JARRY (1873-1907)
UBU ROI (1896)

Various works of Jarry have had a considerable influence on Surrealism; his nonsense-philosophy of 'Pataphysics' is still popular today. Under his precocious genius his schoolboy farces, *King Ubu* and *Ubu Cocu*, flowered from Shakespearean burlesque into a prophecy of dictatorship by a bourgeois-hating anarchist who died of drink at the age of thirty. Ubu's appeal, like Mr Punch's, is universal, he is the Id in action and his anal materialism administered the *coup de grâce* to Des Esseintes. 'You're looking exceptionally plain tonight, Madame Ubu—is it because we have company?' Yeats was saddened by the uproarious first night which he attended with Symons. 'After us', he wrote when he went back to his hotel, 'the savage gods.' Yet even now Jarry is hardly known outside France. His 'Selected Works' edited by Roger Shattuck have just appeared (July 1965).

– 12 HENRY JAMES (1843-1916)
THE AWKWARD AGE
(1899, London)

For this novel about social life in London, said to be modelled on the Asquith circle, James told Logan Pearsall Smith he had invented with infinite thought and wit a new technique of composition and endured endless pains and drudgery 'to give his pages an amusing surface'. The patina of corruption is here something new. Writing in 1918 Pound describes the opening as a *tour de force*, 'a study in punks, a cheese soufflé of the leprous crust of society done to a turn and a niceness save where he puts on the *dolcissimo*, *vox humana* stop. He has pages of clear depiction, even of satire, but the sentimentalist is always lurking round the corner. . . . There is no substitute for narrative sense'. But the sentimentality stays with us too and it is worth mentioning that, in the collected edition, a photograph of his own Lamb House (Rye) was chosen to represent Mr Longdon's unsullied paradise at Beccles.

THE PAX BRITANNICA

The years 1900-14 witnessed a ferment in the arts. Paris led, especially in painting (Cubism from about 1907), London, however, became the capital of prose and remained so till about 1920. French writers grew interested in fantasy, in cosmopolitan sophistication (Larbaud's *Barnabooth*, Gide's *Lafcadio*); their symbol was the amorous millionaire adventurer, cynical and melancholy in his Wagon-lit. Gide founded the *Nouvelle Revue Française*, Rémy de Gourmont edited the *Mercure de France*. Proust retired from the world to prepare his great work. The Irish movement emerged (Moore, Synge), culminating in Yeats' 'Easter 1916'. The deaths (1909) of Meredith and Swinburne left James, Conrad and Hardy supreme by 1910, and the star of Bloomsbury rising. Official religion: sceptical realism (Shaw, Wells, Bennett); official opposition: romantic catholicism (Chesterton, Belloc).

The trial of Oscar Wilde (1895) had left a blight on English literature from which Paris was still immune. The close connection, even the dependence of the men of the Nineties on Paris came to a stop. The Edwardian writers are not closely associated with French painters nor even with English ones. There was nothing to correspond with the Picasso/Apollinaire-Jarry/Bonnard Douanier Rousseau axis or with a literary *cum*-artistic salon like Gertrude Stein's. It is arguable that writers have more to say if they do not derive too much satisfaction from music and painting but nevertheless on literary London—except for the Café Royal—a curtain of provincialism solemnly descends.

13 ANDRÉ GIDE (1869-1951)
L'IMMORALISTE (1902)

'Gide's masterpiece of luminous cruelty' (du Bos). With a construction like an apple peeled in one S-shaped piece Gide dissected the modern pagan (title an allusion to Nietzsche). As Michel's devoted wife nurses her historian husband back to health after a long illness his character grows increasingly harsh and sensual, his proliferating infidelities in the North African climate hasten her own illness and death and he tries in vain to take up history again. Gide's earlier success, *Les Nourritures Terrestres* had more influence on the young but is altogether too vague and syrupy. Here the pagan destructiveness implicit in the pagan obsession with the body, the latent homosexuality which the desert brings out is prophetic of some aspects of his own life, so changed by his meeting with Wilde and Douglas.

- 14 JOSEPH CONRAD (1857-1924)
YOUTH (1902)
- 15 JOSEPH CONRAD
THE SECRET AGENT (1907)

Three stories including 'Heart of Darkness' from which Eliot took the epigraph 'Mistah Kurtz. He dead' for his 'Hollow Men'. This account of a superman running an ivory business in the heart of the Congo for a greedy sanctimonious Belgian company and brutalising himself and the natives in the process, is a masterpiece of sinister deterioration seen by a narrator who is himself profoundly altered by it. (Conrad was for a time captain of a Congo river steamer.) Kurtz is a Dorian Gray whose picture gets a little more frightening with every brush-stroke until in the final scenes everyone within reach—but one—is contaminated.

The Secret Agent depicts the atmosphere of Edwardian London in a psychological thriller of the anarchist underworld. Conrad's wit and chivalrous magnanimity are at their airiest in this novel (beloved of Dr Leavis) which is more influential though less grandly Flaubertian than *Nostromo* (1904) which true Conradians consider his best book. It arose from a little-known *fait-divers* when an Anarchist, Marcel Bourdin, was found blown up by his own explosives near Greenwich Observatory which it was thought he was on his way to destroy (18th February 1894). The Home Secretary described was Sir William Harcourt. Ford claimed to have provided some London topography, but it contains Conrad's greatest heroine and some of the Villiers' '*tendresse exquise*' with his own special hatred of revolutionaries and counter-revolutionaries.

16 HENRY JAMES (1843-1916)
THE AMBASSADORS (1903)

If one starts selecting from James there is no end; it is like choosing an Alp; he dominates the Anglo-American scene for fifty years. *The Ambassadors* is one of his few novels in which European values are clearly shown as preferable to American. 'Quite the best all round, of my productions.' 'Nothing is more easy than to state the subject. "Live all you can: it's a mistake not to."' Besides being his supreme offering to Paris, his renunciation of Puritan America, it is the book in which he considered the form most completely wedded to the content. Pound preferred *The Sacred Fount* where 'he attains form, perfect form, his form.'

17 GEORGE MOORE (1852-1933)
MEMOIRS OF MY DEAD LIFE (1906)

Moore's early *Confessions of a Young Man* are too uneven, too trivial, his *Ave*, *Salve*, *Vale* volumes much too discursive. In these *Memoirs*, which deal with spring in London, Verlaine and Villiers in Paris, and his return to Ireland, and include his charming story *The Lovers of Orelay*, he discovers a seeming-artless style which can glide from narrative to essay and back. Here we hear the true voice of this neglected genius who, had we but patience, is still the best company for depressed insomniacs. A man of such energy and imagination who gave up his whole long life to writing cannot still be ignored and surely awaits resurrection. Alas, he belittled James and Yeats and was cast into outer darkness.

- 18 J. M. SYNGE (1871-1909)
THE PLAYBOY OF THE WESTERN WORLD (1907)

A play which deals light-heartedly with the profound Freudian motive of father-murder, and which therefore outraged the sensitive nationalism of the Irish when it first appeared but immediately became a success in France. Only Synge could truly render spoken Gaelic-Irish into a literary language (*Riders to the Sea*) where Yeats and Moore both failed. *The Playboy* is a comedy which, like all great plays, can be re-read as well as re-visited. Yeats advised Synge, steeped in Mallarmé and Villon, to leave France and employ the speech of the Aran Islanders instead.

19 E. M. FORSTER (b. 1879)
THE LONGEST JOURNEY (1907)

I believe this is Mr Forster's own favourite and I have preferred it to the larger canvas of *Howard's End* (1910), with its patriotic set pieces, despite its gains in subtlety. 'It is the most romantic and passionate of the novels. Everything is felt from the inside.' (Gransden). It opens in the Cambridge of G. E. Moore's *Principia Ethica* (1903), the Cambridge from which Bloomsbury originated, and the book angrily contrasts altruistic undergraduate friendship with the possessiveness of marriage. The title is from Shelley's tirade at monogamy. Another theme, peculiar to Forster, is the reconciliation of the intellectual with the physical, the Don with the child of nature—'only connect'.

- 20 NORMAN DOUGLAS (1868-1952)
SIREN LAND (1911)

A new stage of intimacy in the Anglo-Italian love affair and one of the happiest of travel books. Douglas wrote more ambitiously about Tunisia in *Fountains in the Sand* (1912), and about the South in *Old Calabria* (1915), but they are overladen with digressions and historical information; penetrations in depth but remoter from the Capri-Tiberius-Sirens-Sorrento theme which is central to Douglas's whole literary career. One chapter (on Leisure) was written while he was getting drunk—or claims to have been. Douglas certainly practised the 'refusal of greatness' (which we are told is one of Forster's qualities) throughout his long life. I find his light-hearted intimacy, and delicacy of touch (like Moore's) nearer to the spirit of the Modern Movement than set-pieces such as *Of*

Human Bondage or *The Old Wives' Tale* which reveal so much more construction and narrative power but are so commonplace in their conventional diction.

– 21 D. H. LAWRENCE (1885-1930)
SONS AND LOVERS (1913)

Lawrence strikes out here with the mother-theme after the more rhapsodical first book, *The White Peacock* (1911). His 'Love Poems', 1913, and 'Amores', 1916, form part of the great blossoming of his genius in these three years which include short stories, a play, the Italian sketches and *The Rainbow* (1915-suppressed) and even *Women in Love* finished by 1917 though not published till 1920 (N.Y.) and 1921 (England). His happy period continues till about 1925, with the move to New and Old Mexico and the onset of his illness. Lawrence is a genius whose best work has somehow to be disentangled from the propaganda department of his world reform dictatorship. His message was 'Art for my sake'.

– 22 GUILLAUME APOLLINAIRE (1880-1918)
ALCOOLS

(1913, Paris)

This book of verse by a Polish impresario of mysterious ancestry, interpreter of Cubism, baptiser of Surrealism, novelist, gourmet, bibliophile and pornocrat, includes such modern poems as 'Zone' and the 'Emigrant of Landor Road', and others like the nostalgic '*Le chanson du mal-aimé*' which look back earlier. Steegmuller's recent biography contains some translations (see also *Selected Poems*, Penguin, 1965, translated by Oliver Bernard). By-passing Mallarmé, Apollinaire returned to simpler and fresher forms in the style of Laforgue—and Villon. His imagery is dazzling, his vitality prodigious, his poetry, like Eliot's, both memorable and musical. He believed in a kind of robust sensual sanity quite unlike the more cerebral imagination of the decadents and though always clever and fanciful he can be sometimes shallow and unintelligent. He expended too much of his gift in pot-boiling and marginal creative activity.

23 MARCEL PROUST (1871-1922)
DU CÔTÉ DE CHEZ SWANN (1913)

Translated by Scott Moncrieff as *Swann's Way* etc., Proust's great novel *À la Recherche du temps perdu* is something that happens once in a hundred years like *Les Fleurs du Mal* or *War and Peace*. He combined tragic poetical insight with the gift of creating comic characters in the round, like Shakespeare. He is consistently both intelligent and poetic. Bergsonian philosophy of time gives depth, Ruskinian aesthetics texture. Embittered by his homosexual bias and disabling asthma, he shows some deterioration in the unrevised volumes though not enough to upset this magisterially executed conception of a master-mind in which art erects its monument to dead loves using for material only thought and the passage of time. 'It appeals to our sense of wonder and gains our hommage by its veiled greatness. I don't think there ever has been in the whole of literature such an example of the power of analysis' (Conrad).

It is very much better to read it in French than in the Scott Moncrieff/Sydney Schiff translation in which some of the grandeur evaporates. The Pléiade edition is the best text but the large three-volume Gallimard edition illustrated in colour by Van Dongen is the most satisfactory to handle and the illustrations (though unfair to Charlus) bring out many period details and sometimes whole incidents that one would otherwise miss. The now completed two-volume biography by George Painter (London, Chatto and Windus) restores to us the lead in Proustian research.

24 W. B. YEATS (1865-1939)
RESPONSIBILITIES
(1914, Dublin; enlarged, 1916, London)

In these poems Yeats, influenced by his young secretary Pound, breaks away from his early manner and begins to purge his imagery of abstraction and to write more simply and directly, achieving mastery in *Michael Robartes and the Dancer* and *The Wild Swans at Coole* which followed. The new note sounds in the first poem in which he shakes off the onus of his unrequited love for Maud Gonne.

> Pardon that for a barren passion's sake
> Although I have come close on forty-nine
> I have no child, I have nothing but a book . . .

1914-1918

THE war dislocated the Modern Movement but did not destroy it. Some lost their faith in humanity, many were killed; nearly all had to cease writing. War poetry boomed while the spirit of revolt against the older generation grew more ominous (Sassoon, 1918, *Counter-Attack*). Of the three major war-poets Sassoon was the most conventional, depending on epigrams with a sting in the tail, Isaac Rosenberg (a private soldier from the East End) was the most original but the most unskilled in the handling of verse and only Wilfrid Owen combined technical resource with profound feeling. Many war experiences were digested later while some of the best writing remained, in spirit anyhow, pre-war and was carried on in isolated back-waters (Joyce in Trieste and Zürich, Firbank in Oxford, Lawrence in Cornwall, Strachey and other pacifists on farms). The war, self-destruction of a golden civilisation, was for most writers an intense and crippling disillusion, an interval for killing, dying, hating and lying. Many fell silent by the time they had apprehended the universal slaughter house to which they had been led.

---

25 THOMAS HARDY (1840-1928)
SATIRES OF CIRCUMSTANCE (1914)

The 'Satires' in this book link Hardy more directly to the Movement than his novels, which had all been steeped in the Victorian tradition. They are Maupassant-like vignettes passed through his great contemplative soul and they strike a new note like the poems about his dead wife in the same volume which concludes with the first war-poem, 'Men who march away', and contains his much more remarkable poem about the sinking of the *Titanic*—'The Convergence of the Twain.'

26 JAMES JOYCE (1882-1941)
PORTRAIT OF THE ARTIST AS A YOUNG MAN

(1916, New York; 1917, London)

Stephen Dedalus describes his spiritual journey through his Jesuit education and petty bourgeois Dublin to forge through 'silence, exile and cunning' the 'uncreated conscience of his race'. Following close on *Dubliners* (for it appeared through 1915 as a serial in *The Egoist*) the Portrait can be read either as an autobiography or a novel. A landmark in sensibility, the prose moves forward in complexity from the child's sensations at the beginning to the adolescent subtleties at the end. An interesting earlier version, *Stephen Hero*, was published in 1944 by Cape and New Directions.

27 FORD MADOX FORD (1873-1939)
THE GOOD SOLDIER (1915)

'The best French novel in the English language' (Rodker). There is a reserve tank of energy and intelligence about this most subtle study of the eternal quadrilateral (two couples meeting in a German Spa) which sets it apart from the over-written romanticism of his Tietjens war trilogy. [Originally called 'The Saddest Story'.] Ford's romantic snobbery and irrepressible egotism are here still under control—and James and Flaubert provide that control. Ford ('Fordie') has an honourable record in the Movement. He founded the *English Review* (1908) and befriended and published Lawrence, Pound, Norman Douglas; and in 1923 he edited *Trans-atlantic Review* which published Hemingway's stories with

Joyce under the title *Work in Progress*. He wrote several autobiographies with reminiscences of James and Conrad and ended up in America, dying in Deauville, 1939. 'You were a kind man and you died in want' (Lowell).

– 28 NORMAN DOUGLAS (1868-1952)
SOUTH WIND (1917)

One cannot re-read *South Wind* without stumbling over cairns of boredom (Keith, one gathers, was intended to be a bore—sometimes—and the discursions and digressions often make it worse)—yet it is an astonishingly civilised and good-humoured book, full of Douglas's sanity and cobweb-sweeping charm. It contains the first futile young man, a ''Twenties' prototype, and his rival, a typical redbrick young scientist. Even though we do have to dip and skip it is far better than those contemporary autobiographical novels; pantechnicons of indulgent self-ness. 'I find everything useful and nothing indispensable. I find everything wonderful and nothing miraculous. I reverence the body. I avoid first causes like the plague,' says Keith. (Aldington here detects the influence of Wilde and in *Pinorman* has delivered a snide attack on the book, which he sees as a derivative of Wilde and Moore; but *South Wind* survives because it pleases, because Douglas's cackle is still infectious.)

29 PERCY WYNDHAM LEWIS (1886-1957)
TARR

(1918, New York and London)

'Written much earlier' (by 1914), re-written in the nineteen-twenties. Artists in Paris, not idealised as by Moore, but situated in the hey-day of Montparnasse with its parasitic Poles and vociferous Germans. A new note is present, the unsentimental, the objective pictorial fragmentation of the human face and body with its activities like the laugh, which reminds one of Cubist painting. The gains in Lewis's later work are offset by corresponding losses. Thus here and in the stories of *The Wild Body* (same period) he crackles and coruscates without trying, as in his later work, to prove himself a great moral philosopher and avenger or, as in his critical books, protesting like an elephant picking over a dustbin. Eliot called Lewis the greatest journalist he knew, and by this implication he was also the most frustrated artist, a hard-boiled Haydon.

30 T. S. ELIOT (1888-1965)

(*a*) *PRUFROCK AND OTHER OBSERVATIONS*

(1917, *The Egoist*)

Reprinted in *Collected Poems*, 1909-25, *Collected Poems*, 1936, etc. Contains the 'Love Song' and the disturbing 'Preludes' and 'Rhapsody' (written in Paris and published by Lewis in *Blast*), something quite new in English verse and far beyond the capacity of Laforgue who is given credit for influencing him. '*Le frisson nouveau*' that Hugo remarked in Baudelaire is found in these magically recorded moments of polite futility set against the mounting urban horror. 'Here was a protest and a feeble one and the more congenial for being feeble. . . .' —'He who could turn aside to complain of ladies or drawing rooms preserved a tiny drop of our self-respect' (E. M. Forster).

(*b*) *THE WASTE LAND*

(1922, New York; 1923, London)

Reprinted with 'Prufrock' in *Poems*, 1909-25, 1909-35, etc. Becoming as hard to obtain as 'Prufrock'; it is better to search for the *Poems* 1909-25, perhaps his most important book. Of *The Waste Land* I will say nothing but that we should read it every April. It is the breviary of post-war disillusion, 'the hope only of empty men', written in Switzerland after a near break-down, pruned of some connecting passages (including a ship-wreck) by Pound, and as Adrienne Monnier wrote of Pelléas, hard to listen to without tears—'*si mystérieusement émouvante*'. 'Eliot's *Waste Land* is I think the justification of the modern experiment since 1900' (Pound).

31 PAUL VALÉRY (1871-1945)

(*a*) *LA JEUNE PARQUE* (1917)

Reprinted in *Poésies*, 1942. Translated by Charles Davy in 'Words in the Mind', Chatto, 1965. Here Valéry broke his long silence of twenty years. (The incomparable 'Evening with M. Teste' had appeared only in a magazine, 1896.) This, like all his best poetry is about the act of creation. Here he leads the Alexandrine away from Mallarmé's inner reverie and contrives a Racinian mastery of the long sentence. A poet's poem which Thibaudet, Larbaud and other war-weary enthusiasts learnt by heart when it came out in a small edition, dedicated to André Gide. 'The most difficult poem in the French language.' It is not, however, necessary altogether to understand it as its exquisite musical monotonies (like Debussy again) induce a trance. Valéry considered it a true picture of the emotional awakening of a young girl, or rather goddess. '*Le sujet vague de l'oeuvre est la conscience de soi-même. La "Consciousness" de Poesi l'on veut*'—see his key letter to Mockel.

(*b*) *CHARMES* (1922)

(*Poésies*, 1942.) This collection contains his greatest poem '*Le Cimetière Marin*' (the Gray's Elegy of my generation) whose conclusion, '*Il faut tenter de vivre*', provides the answer to the Prufrock-Waste Land death wish. The title, *Charmes*, can mean 'hornbeams' or 'incantations' and the shorter poems include the magical '*Les Pas*', 'The Steps'. Henceforth Valéry was gradually to retire into prose to become the foremost man of letters of his day (*Variété* 1-5 and many other books of creative criticism). Valéry was born at Sète and is buried in his mother's family vault (Grassi) in the 'graveyard by the sea'—his epitaph two lines from it:

> *O récompense après une pensée*
> *qu'un long regard sur le calme des Dieux.*

–32 GUILLAUME APOLLINAIRE (1880-1918)

CALLIGRAMMES (1918)

From being an intellectual Diaghilev, an entrepreneur between poetry and painting, Apollinaire flung himself vigorously into the great war; he was wounded, trepanned and died of Spanish 'flu within a week of Wilfred Owen (November 1918). Some of the best war-poems in any language are to be found here together with experiments like '*Les Fenêtres*' (Cubist) and '*La Jolie Rousse*', which were far ahead of their time. The *Calligrammes* themselves (Pattern Poems) are less interesting than some of the others when copied out straight.

33 GERARD MANLEY HOPKINS (1844-1889)

POEMS (1918)

Edited by Bridges (enlarged 1930). Though written in the 'seventies and 'eighties in the case of the tragic sonnets, these extraordinary poems which incorporated the metrical device of 'sprung rhythm' still took time to circulate and influenced the poets of the 'thirties, rather than the Georgians. The first reviews were almost all unfriendly. 'He must remain a poet's poet' (Murry, 1919). Praise came from Dr Richards (*Dial*, 1926), Graves and Riding (1927), Empson (1930), Leavis (1932), Read (1933), Edith Sitwell and Eliot (1934). *The Notebooks and Correspondence of Hopkins* (1937) complete the revelation of this inspired Jesuit priest for so long ignored. Hopkins's poetry with its religious faith, his experiments in versification, his 'dark night of the soul' would have reduced all his Victorian contemporaries to immediate insignificance—like Rimbaud's in France—had they but known of him.

34 ARTHUR WALEY (b. 1889)

ONE HUNDRED AND SEVENTY CHINESE POEMS (1918)

'A beautiful place is the town of Lo-Yang'

Reprinted with all his other Chinese poems in 1946. In 1915 Pound in *Cathay* had applied imagism to Chinese verse. Waley was an accurate scholar as well and brought a whole civilisation into English poetry, as he was to bring another one, a second time, into prose with the Japanese *Tale of Genji*. Today the poems are as necessary and haunting as ever and enshrine the ethical values of G. E. Moore (aesthetic experiences + personal relations = the good life) though remaining intrinsically Chinese. While the lyrical and bibulous Li-Po comes down to us through many translations, one might claim that the more reflective Po-Chui is the private creation of Waley. . . .

'Paulownia flowers just on the point of falling
are a symbol to express "thinking of an absent friend".'

35 EZRA POUND (b. 1885)

(*a*) *LUSTRA* (1916) & (*b*) *MAUBERLEY* (1920)

Reprinted in *Selected Poems*, chosen by Eliot (1928). (*Lustra* includes *Cathay*.) An active organiser rather than an introvert like Eliot, Pound had written half a dozen books by 1916. *Lustra*, apart from some troubadour poems, is mostly a collection of arrogant epigrams and light-hearted Catullus-like lyrics in imagist-fantasist style. He bade farewell to England in 1920 in the highly artificial, musical and sardonic poems of *Mauberley*. *Mauberley* is a somewhat effete Jamesian hero disgruntled by the London rat-race, wandering through the drawing-room jungles where Pound had once trumpeted. 'His true Penelope was Flaubert.' The Poems are short harpsichord pieces combining melancholy with anger and they provide, with 'Homage to Sextus Propertius' (1919), a kaleidoscope of imperial decay, the changing hues of the dying mullet.

Critics, concentrating on the allusive sophistication of *Mauberley* and its polished quatrains, are apt to ignore the violent passions underlying its 'defunctive music' and emerging in the anti-war poem:

Died some, *pro patria*,
non 'dulce' non 'et decor' . . .

Walked eye-deep in hell
believing in old men's lies, then unbelieving
come home, home to a lie,
home to many deceits
home to old lies and new infamy; . . .

Daring as never before, wastage as never before
Young blood and high blood,
fair cheeks and fine bodies;
fortitude as never before
frankness as never before
disillusions as never told in the old days
hysterias, trench confessions,
laughter out of dead bellies. . . .

36 WILFRED OWEN (1893-1918)

POEMS

Edited by Siegfried Sassoon, 1920 (reprinted and expanded). Owen, who was killed in the very last week of the war, had the genius to come through the rage and frustration or even the dearth of feeling of many war-poets and so to write the first understanding poems about the shell-shocked, about gas, about the enemy. His loss and that of Isaac Rosenberg—'*quick eyes gone under earth's lid*'—were disasters, examples of war's wasteful uselessness (for they died while their talents were taking great strides forward). Owen was influenced by his French friend, the *fantaisiste* Laurent Tailhade, whom he knew in his youth at Bordeaux. His present fashion is no accident but the tardy recognition of his compelling superiority, first recognised by the young poets of the 'thirties and by his friend Osbert Sitwell, though denied by Yeats.

- 37 LYTTON STRACHEY (1880-1932)
EMINENT VICTORIANS (1918)

It might be described as the first book of the 'twenties. Strachey (who was born in the year George Eliot died) was engaged not only in trimming the fat off the Victorians, he applied his ironical attitude to humanity in general. Yet underneath the sceptic and scholar flamed a passionate Elizabethan. He struck the note of ridicule which the whole war-weary generation wanted to hear, using the weapon of Bayle, Voltaire and Gibbon on the creators of the Red Cross and the Public School System. It appeared to the post-war young people like the light at the end of a tunnel.

PART II

1920-1930

THE 'TWENTIES

THE essential quality of the 'twenties was release from strain, enthusiasm for experiment, hope for the future. It was the age of the Intellectual Mannerists: Douglas, Strachey, Pearsall Smith, Firbank, Van Vechten, Huxley, the Sitwells; of Cocteau, Morand, Fargue and Giraudoux; of brilliant women writers, Edith Sitwell, Virginia Woolf, Colette, Katherine Mansfield, Edith Wharton, Willa Cather and Gertrude Stein. Travel became a ruling passion. The first half of the decade was the more exuberant and 1922 has been described by R. P. Blakmur as an Annus Mirabilis. Demobilised American writers, fugitives from Prohibition and the Family Business, began to assert themselves as the centre shifted from London to Paris while Surrealism appeared with Breton's first *Manifesto* of 1924. The Café made way for the Night Club. In the last half of the decade the sense of liberation turned to increasing apprehension. The slump of 1929 was a time of suicides and conversions. War memoirs abounded, Wyndham Lewis wrote his early eulogy of Hitler (1930). The great frost of '29 drove the Expatriates home, shorn of their private incomes, restoring the Left Bank to Gide and Valéry.

It was a joy then to be alive. The 'twenties had something of the 'nineties about them in that there was still room for the *culte du moi*. Writers were not regimented, criticism was largely amateur, Eng.Litt. was something, in which Aldous Huxley had got a First, that went up as far as Chaucer. The afternoon train would land one in Paris on the spur of the moment and the cafés were crowded and living cheap. Each left-bank hotel harboured a memorable face—from Anderson to Westcott—and all were to be met with at Sylvia Beach's lending library. Germany was another adventure, and Italy or Spain. (One could live in Spain on ten shillings a day.) James was dead and Proust was dying but there were still great writers to be seen who were also fascinating—like Joyce and Lawrence—and young groups round the Sitwells or Gide or Breton or Strachey for whom everything seemed possible and all barriers down.

---

38 D. H. LAWRENCE (1885-1930)
SEA AND SARDINIA
(1921, New York; 1923, London)

'Comes over one an absolute necessity to move.' The first words might be a motto for the period. The whole book is one long dithyrambic ecstasy written at the height of his passion for Freda and contemporary with the charming poems of the 'Birds, beasts and flowers' cycle. It was Lawrence's second book about Italy and full of his feeling for the Tyrrhenian and for primitive peoples. Italy was still a war-torn country, as can be seen from Douglas's astringent *Alone* (same year). 'A book of about three hundred pages, written in six weeks, containing the experiences of two poor people—and it is magical' (Aldington). Lawrence never marinates his travel books in historical digressions: one is always on the move with him, seeing with him, living in the present.

39 ALDOUS HUXLEY (1894-1963)
CROME YELLOW (1921)

Early Huxley ends with *Antic Hay* (1923), a 'must' for the period but not as fresh and startling as the stories in *Limbo* and *Mortal Coils*, or this radiant conversation-piece about the first 'bright young people', gathered round Lady Ottoline Morrell at Garsington. (Mr Wimbush however bears a resemblance to Sir George Sitwell.) Typical ineffectual mannerist hero like Denis in *South Wind*, but not yet cynical. One does not yet hear the rattling of the cerebral donkey engine which drowns his later prose. Peacock is still in the ascendant, the moralising pundits have not taken over. The 'amusing surface' for which James strove nearly always eludes Huxley, perhaps he did not even desire it, but it is found here while the crust in *Antic Hay* is already soggy.

- 40 KATHERINE MANSFIELD (1890-1923)
THE GARDEN PARTY (1922)

Her best book of stories, surpassing in airy freshness even the Huxley of *Crome Yellow*. He was to describe her, not too sympathetically, in *Those Barren Leaves*. She also figures in Isherwood's novel, *The World in the Evening*. This is feminine writing at its best, and her friend Virginia Woolf could not improve on such impressionism. A born short story writer, observant, economical and astringent, demanding rediscovery. Her letters and journals, edited by her husband, Middleton Murry, are still good reading. She died of consumption like Lawrence, Beardsley and Orwell; New Zealand's only offering to our avant-garde.

41 W. B. YEATS (1865-1939)
LATER POEMS (1922)

Contains in one volume all his work from *The Wind among the Reeds* through *The Wild Swans at Coole* and *Michael Robartes and the Dancer*. *The Wind among the Reeds* is the culmination of his Celtic Twilight Morris manner, 'the swan-song of his fin-de-siècle compositions' (Jeffares). Influenced by Symons' translations of Mallarmé, he described these poems as 'wavering organic rhythms which are the embodiment of the imagination'. One should try to possess all these books in the Dublin limited editions to study the development of the greatest poet of the century. Thus at Easter 1916 he was engrossed in the Japanese *No Plays*, with Ezra Pound. The great patriotic poem came six months later. In this same year, 1922, appeared his marvellous autobiography, *The Trembling of the Veil*. We now know how much concentrated revision went into all his poems and his whole output gives the lie to those who propound that a poet is all the better for another job. His often eccentric course of reading developed through prolonged meditation a set of ideas and images which glow through the deceptive simplicity of his verse forms and render his lightest song elusively.

In this volume, still easy to obtain and a delight to the eye, we can trace his last 'poems for poetry's sake' through the realism of *Galway Races* and the political '*Poems written in discouragement*' of 1913 to the new directness of *The Wild Swans at Coole*.

42 JAMES JOYCE (1882-1941)

ULYSSES

(1922, Paris)

Ulysses is not a great novel in the sense of *Á la recherche du temps perdu*. The characters do not develop. It has no consistent tragic grandeur and bogs down in several stylistic exercises which have nothing to do with the novel proper; yet the early Dedalus sections, the middle parts of Bloom and the Nightown orgy and Molly's final reverie stand out like

Gaudi's unfinished cathedral. The whole plan fails through Joyce's intellectual preference for language rather than people—yet somehow it does achieve greatness like a ruined temple soaring from a jungle—and should be judged perhaps as a poem, a festival of the imagination. It is also *our* novel, adopted at last even by Ireland and begetter of several generations of theses in America. Bloom is a universal comic character like Falstaff, Dedalus is guilty adolescence and even though we do not pursue the symbolism, colour charts, and all the extrapolations adumbrated by Stuart Gilbert and others, we can all partake of the etched perfection of the early chapters and the gathering momentum of father lost and father found. 'All the fuggs, all the foetors, the whole boil of the European mind had been lanced' [Ezra Pound].

43 RAYMOND RADIGUET (1903-1923)
LE DIABLE AU CORPS (1923)

Translated, *The Devil in the Flesh*, by Kay Boyle (Grey Walls Press). Written when he was seventeen, this first novel burst like a bombshell; an absolutely direct and truthful but far from superficial account of a love-affair between a schoolboy and a married woman whose husband was in the trenches. (The husband only discovered the truth when informed late in life by a journalist.) Radiguet died aged twenty of pneumonia after writing a neo-classical novel, *Le Bal du Comte d'Orgel* in accordance with the Cocteau-Stravinsky '*retour à l'ordre*'. I prefer *Le Diable* to those other famous love-stories, *Le Grand Meaulnes* (1914), whose other-worldliness becomes too laboured, and *Bubu of Montparnasse*.

44 RONALD FIRBANK (1886-1926)
THE FLOWER BENEATH THE FOOT (1923)

Firbank's novels, owning allegiance only to Congreve, had been appearing steadily through the war years, financed by himself. Superficially an orchidaceous dandy with a private income he was at heart more than an aesthete, a solitary hard-working dedicated perfectionist. *The Flower* (which lacks the compulsive didacticism of *Antic Hay*—same year) is more exotic and assured than his earlier work that seems indeed to be leading up to it. It combines impressionist word-painting, elusive dialogue with a wisp of devotional fragrance. Less 'camp' than *Prancing Nigger* or *the Eccentricities of Cardinal Pirelli*, it is, of all his books, the worthiest of Forster's praise and Auden's passionate admiration.

-45 E. M. FORSTER (b. 1879)
A PASSAGE TO INDIA (1924)

Begun many years earlier, Forster's great novel bridges the Edwardian-Georgian era. The Mahommedan Aziz, the Hindu Dr Godbole, the emancipated Englishman Fielding and the sibylline Mrs Moore are his most complete creations against a crisis that is emotionally experienced and also worked out ethically and philosophically. Forster explored the limitations of humanism and the world beyond and beneath it just before Lawrence tried to annihilate humanism altogether. His solution comes nearer to Huxley's but his visual sense is given over to delight rather than to salvation through nausea. The novel bade us leave India gracefully, and so we left. 'A miracle of intelligence, tact, irony, prudence and ability' (André Gide).

46 WALLACE STEVENS (1879-1955)
HARMONIUM (1923)

Reprinted in *Collected Poems*. Enter America. Stevens was over forty when his first book, containing much of his best work, was published. He takes delicious liberties with the American idiom, he radiates sensuous happiness and verbal felicity especially in his shorter poems. Although not an expatriate, he was deeply influenced by Laforgue and Mallarmé and his vision has been compared to Matisse. His most solid work is considered to be the much later *Transport to Summer*, but here he makes his impact with 'Peter Quince at the Clavier' and his celebrated 'Sunday Morning'. He remained in Hartford, Connecticut all his life in the Insurance Company of which he became vice-president, not without side-effects.

47 E. E. CUMMINGS (1894-1962)
(*a*) *TULIPS & CHIMNEYS* (1923 & 1937)
(*b*) *Is 5* (1926, New York)

Both reprinted in *Collected Poems* (1938). In the same year as Frost's traditional masterpiece, *New Hampshire*, appeared the unconventional Harvard-Bowery-Paris volume of *Tulips & Chimneys* which the publishers broke up into three books, reunited in the edition of 1937. The erotic poems were privately printed in *And* (1925), another fragment *41 Poems* (1925) won the Dial Prize (awarded Eliot, 1922; Marianne Moore, 1924). Cummings remained in full spate up to 1926 with *Is 5* (his fifth book, counting his war novel, *The Enormous Room*). Cummings is far more like Catullus than is Pound; his realistic cityscapes and speakeasy poems (reward of repatriation) are exciting and original 'so quite new a thing'—like his fierce love poetry and satires (when not too anarcho-sentimental). The years 1920-25 were for him one long manic outpouring of passion, contempt and the joy of living. His typographical capers freshen his otherwise conventional verse forms, but sometimes pall. Of all the members of the American avant-garde who did not die young like Crane or West, Cummings remained the most *dans le vrai*, the most consistent and uncompromising in his adherence to the Baudelairean concept of the poetic life—without honours or possessions or remunerative side-lines, intolerant of all false situations, keeping in training for the visitations of the Muse who did not abandon him. Some of his best poems are in *One Times One* (1944) and later.

48 SCOTT FITZGERALD (1896-1940)
THE GREAT GATSBY (1925)

Fitzgerald reached a large public with *This Side of Paradise* (1920); an adolescent collegiate best-seller influenced by Rupert Brooke and Compton Mackenzie. It is all the more to his credit that he should have moved on to this light-hearted masterpiece of the boom years (one of the half-dozen best American novels) which won the instant acclaim of Eliot. There is evidence of weakness and there are shifts of emphasis in 'Gatsby', but it remains a prose poem of delight and sadness which has by now introduced two generations to the romance of America, as *Huckleberry Finn* and *Leaves of Grass* introduced those before it.

49 ERNEST HEMINGWAY (1899-1961)
IN OUR TIME
(1924, Paris; 1925 and 1930, New York)

50 ERNEST HEMINGWAY
THE SUN ALSO RISES
(1926, New York)

The emergence of Hemingway, influenced by *Huckleberry Finn*, Gertrude Stein (*Three Lives*, 1909) and Sherwood Anderson (*Winesburg, Ohio*, 1918) gave the Modern Movement one of its few men of action, like Malraux and Saint Exupéry. *In Our Time* is a sequence of father-haunted short stories about the author's boyhood in Michigan, counterpointed by prose poems depicting the horrors of war. In later editions more stories were added but the structure, the growing up of Nick into the macabre world of the war vignettes until they merge, remains unaltered. Other stories like 'The Undefeated' and 'Hills like White Elephants' followed rapidly and then the short picaresque novel *The Sun also Rises* (English title *Fiesta*), to which a suppressed first chapter has just been published. Here the post-war disillusion and the post-war liberation are united in the physical enjoyment of living and the pains of love. Perhaps that is what expatriation was about. The combined effect of these two books and the short stories (afterwards to become *Men without Women*) was overwhelming. No other writer here recorded stepped so suddenly into fame, or destroyed with such insouciance so many other writers or ways of writing or became such an immediate symbol of an age.

51 ANDRÉ GIDE (1869-1951)

SI LE GRAIN NE MEURT

(1920 onwards in the N.R.F. magazine—Published Paris, 1926)

Translated *If it die* by Dorothy Bussy (Modern Library, New York, and Secker). Gide's autobiography is a work of art or rather the true portrait of the artist as a young man, for his horizon was much larger than Joyce's and he writes with an electric excitement. Financially independent, he came of a long line of Protestants, Catholic on his mother's side, with his roots in Nîmes and Normandy. His mother's influence was decisive. It is not only the story of a young man escaping from his family but of the discovery of his homosexual tastes, the first of its kind in history to reveal such experiences in the first person (encouraged in this by Proust, see his *Journal*). Gide in 1911 had written *Corydon* to prove that homosexuality was not against nature, but nothing there is comparable to the absorbing account of his initiation by Wilde and Douglas at Biskra, the shock of self-knowledge abruptly coinciding with his platonic marriage to his cousin.

52 WILLIAM PLOMER (b. 1903)

TURBOTT WOLFE (1926, dated 1925)

Reprinted with a new foreword by Laurens Van der Post, 1965. Born in 1903, Plomer wrote his first novel (also his first book) with a charming dandyism suggesting both Forster and Firbank, but the theme is far from frivolous and states the South African colour problem as realistically as it has ever been treated since. There is even a mixed marriage. The English liberals, the old settlers, the church, the poor whites, the Afrikaner and the African are vividly described and their passions spin the plot. 'Awoke a sleepy continent to rage' (Roy Campbell).

- 53 SOMERSET MAUGHAM (b. 1874)
THE CASUARINA TREE (1926)

Although influenced by Maupassant, most of Maugham's work is traditional rather than modern and Georgian prose-poetical passages abound. In these Far Eastern short stories ('The Casuarina Tree' and 'Ah King') and in the secret service tales of *Ashenden* (1928), Maugham achieves an unspoken ferocity, a controlled ruthlessness before returning to sentiment with Rosie in *Cakes and Ale*. He tells us—and it had not been said before—exactly what the British in the Far East were like, the judges and planters and civil servants and their womenfolk at home, even as *Ashenden* exposes what secret service work is really like. That would not be enough without his mastery of form, if not of language. His bloodless annexation of the Far East pays off in *The Casuarina Tree* which includes 'The Yellow Streak', 'The Out Station', 'Before the Party' and 'The Letter'—about a coward, a snob, a murderess and a blackmailer.

-54 VIRGINIA WOOLF (1882-1941)
TO THE LIGHTHOUSE (1927)

One of her few novels where something happens, written at the height of her luminous Impressionist vision. The lighthouse was near St Ives though the story is set in Scotland and is about her father, Sir Leslie Stephen, and the world round her mother and her aunt, the photographer, Mrs

Cameron. It is the sunniest of her books and shows the obsession with rendering the passage of time which dominated her later work. With her prosperous upper middle class academic background of the late Victorian establishment Virginia Woolf is always walking a tight-rope in her desire to get away from it and portray ordinary people as a novelist should, hence the mixture of respect and irony with which she surveys its security and solid values. Sometimes she diverges into fantasies about charwomen which don't come off, or into uncritical acceptance of her social advantages. But a central undomesticated bleakness saves her.

55 ANDRÉ BRETON (b. 1896)
NADJA (1928)

Translated by Richard Howard (Grove Press, 1964). Surrealism arrived out of Dada with Breton's *Manifesto* of 1924. A romantic-revolutionary movement, it encompassed all the arts though losing some of its exponents (Aragon, Eluard) to Communism. Its high-spots were the paintings and collages of Max Ernst (*La Semaine de Bonté*) and the films of Buñuel, and it influenced certain English poets (Gascoyne, Dylan Thomas) and many painters. It stemmed from Central European nihilistic defeatism (Dada) and the satanically romantic Lautréamont and also Rimbaud. Nothing more Surrealist has ever been written than Lautréamont's: 'beautiful as the chance encounter on a dissecting table of an umbrella and a sewing-machine'. Breton, the *chef d'école* of the Movement who proposed to 'wring the neck of literature' owes much to his friendship with Jacques Vaché (1916), 'Nadja' (1926) and Trotsky. His style is dense; fortuitous meetings, coincidences and juxtapositions fill him with awe and wonder '*La beauté sera convulsive ou ne sera pas*'. *Nadja* derives something from the dream-stories of Nerval, and evokes a friendship with a mediumistic White Russian girl through a series of haphazard encounters, '*le merveilleux du quotidien*' dear to the Surrealist imagination. She wound up in an asylum. *Nadja* is however considered by some to be a muse or state of mind. Another important book: *Les Pas Perdus*, 1924, contains Breton's first surrealist art-criticism and his essay on Apollinaire. Aragon's brilliant *Paysan de Paris* (1926) is another such 'anti-novel'. Breton never became a Communist and has remained true to the dictates of the personal revolution which he founded with his cry of '*changez la vie!*'

56 W. B. YEATS (1865-1939)

(*a*) *THE TOWER*

(1928, London)

(*b*) *THE WINDING STAIR*

(1929, New York; enlarged 1933, London)

'The calm of evening, Lissadell' . . .

These two volumes contain the greatest poetry of Yeats in his difficult later manner ('Sailing to Byzantium'). They constitute a peak in English poetry. Yeats, however complicated his thought, remained a consummate musician in his expression of it as can be seen from 'In Memory of Eva Gore-Booth, and Con Markiewicz' which opens *The Winding Stair*. In *Words for Music Perhaps* and the subsequent volumes the shorter lyrics show a slight falling off in intensity. I have given the dates of the London editions; the collector will prefer *October Blast* (1927, Dublin) to *The Tower* and look for the American *Winding Stair*. One is tempted to include the prose *A Packet for Ezra Pound* (Dublin 1929) as well.

– 57 D. H. LAWRENCE (1885-1930)
LADY CHATTERLEY'S LOVER
(1928, Florence)

'Mr Lawrence has moments of greatness, of course, but hours of something very different' wrote Virginia Woolf (*The Common Reader*). His 'passionate messianic' didacticism mars many of his novels and is kept under better control in the long-short stories or short novels (*The Fox*, *St Mawr*, and *The Man who Died*). It mars *Lady Chatterley*, which is a puritanical tract on the art of love as Lawrence imagined it, devised to rouse the English from their torpor. Lawrence fully intended to shock and expected his book to be banned. The time-bomb only recently exploded when the issue of the trial ended censorship in England. Should be read in conjunction with his letters (edited by Aldous Huxley). Even without the eroticism it is a fascinating and well-planned novel rich in post-war observation and character portrait.

– 58 EVELYN WAUGH (b. 1903)
DECLINE AND FALL (1928)

Waugh afterwards departed from the Modern Movement and became a novelist in the Catholic tradition, but one can at no time say that he entirely forsook his early ideal exemplified by the modern architect in *Decline and Fall. Black Mischief* and *Scoop* retain something of the old avant-garde Adam and so does his *The Loved One* (1948). *Decline and Fall* and *Vile Bodies* are, however, anarchic and experimental and the former is surely one of the wittiest and most original of first novels (*aetatis suae* 25). Champagne to the particular. Amorality diminishes, circa 1934, with *A Handful of Dust.*

59 HENRY GREEN (b. 1905)
LIVING
(1929, London)

Living is a novel about a family business (paternal-proletarian)—an engineering works in Birmingham which a young man takes over from his dying father. But, despite the delicious satire on his position and love affairs, the book is really about skilled craftsmen, foremen and works managers in a phase of industrial depression. The main characters are a girl, Lily and her two admirers, and her grandfather, Craigan, a moulder. Written (his second book) by a young man of twenty-four, it is a work of astonishing maturity and brilliance, showing a complete mastery of unfamiliar speech rhythms and a grasp of working-class character, especially of the sixty-year olds, who are so set in their ways, yet so afraid of the future. It is also a poetic novel, rich in unusual imagery and juxtapositions and with a bubbling and lacerating wit, often at the young man's expense. The new broom sweeps far from clean, the living are also the loving and foredoomed: 'We are imprisoned by that person whom we love'. Henry Green went on to write many novels, mostly about his own milieu, except for *Loving* (1945), about the servants in an empty Irish house in war-time, but reveal none so sure an ear as in *Living*, nor such exuberant talents.

60 ERNEST HEMINGWAY (1899-1961)

A FAREWELL TO ARMS (1929)

His first full-length novel and probably his best, closely rivalled by *To Have and Have Not* (1937). Its success was so enormous that it may be said to have ended Hemingway's influence as a writer. After it one could no more imitate that musical crystal-clear style; blown like glass from the white-heat of violence. He returned to the Caporetto scene in *Across the River and Into the Trees* (1950). We are told of immense labours over the last sentence: the beginning, like all his beginnings, seems effortless and magical. Here, for the first time, his inability to create three-dimensional heroines appears a defect. Here too he becomes painfully aware of all that is expected of him.

61 ROBERT GRAVES (b. 1895)

GOODBYE TO ALL THAT (1929)

It is regrettable that so few autobiographies are works of art, they are nearly always overloaded with discursive case-history. Graves both describes the growth of a poet's mind and gives an objective picture of trench-warfare, ending with his total renunciation of the post-war English scene ten years after Pound's. The same year he printed his remarkable *Poems 1929*, before retiring to Majorca with Laura Riding, thus joining the Modern Movement at an age when others leave it. The first edition contains a poem of Sassoon's afterwards suppressed. But did he remain a modern? After some indecision one concludes that when he emerged from the Riding school, he returned to traditionalism, with no admiration for Eliot, Pound or Yeats. His remarkable recent poems come too late so here—in 1929—we bid farewell to him regretfully.

62 JEAN COCTEAU (1891-1963)
LES ENFANTS TERRIBLES (1929)

(Translated with a foreword by Rosamond Lehmann as 'Children of the game')

Although I know that Cocteau demands a place, I cannot altogether repress a wish to keep him out to make room for something less self-conscious like the *Histoire de l'Oeil*, a tale of pure pornography with which the young Georges Bataille, under the pseudonym of Lord Auch, graduate of Oxford and Cambridge, burst on an astonished though limited world in 1929. But Cocteau, wittiest and kindest of men, was at the heart of the Paris avant-garde from before 1914. He takes over immediately from Apollinaire. His *Opium* and *Retour à l'ordre* once gave me deep pleasure. Yet Cocteau's earlier poetry, books of criticism and opium experiences just fail to add up to a masterpiece. *Le Potomak* and *Thomas l'Imposteur* are perhaps the best, but in this novel about the cruelty and beauty (both unconscious) of teenagers and the dream-world congruity of a brother and sister, his metallic brilliance triumphs. Fame as a dramatist is just round the corner. The hard-centred snow-ball thrown by the handsome Dargelos becomes a favourite symbol and joins the obsessional cluster of images which remain ceaselessly in orbit round the impresario-poet.

63 IVY. COMPTON BURNETT (b. 1892)
BROTHERS AND SISTERS (1929)

Miss Compton Burnett's novels have been so long with us that one forgets that there was a time when they had a beginning (*Dolores*, 1911). *Pastors and Masters*, 1925 was her second book, but *Brothers and Sisters* with its theme of incest, is her 'first entirely achieved and satisfactory novel' (Burkhart). The pattern is now set: Scarlatti-like dialogue, atrocious crimes, tyranny enthroned in the bosom of the family, the Victorian paterfamilias as a root of all evil and justice proceeding ineluctably as in her favourite models in Greek tragedy. All her characters, whatever their station, insist upon the pleasure of expressing themselves perfectly.

– 64 HART CRANE (1899-1932)
THE BRIDGE

(January 1930, Paris; 1930, New York)

Crane (Harold was changed to Hart) had been publishing poems since the war years; his first book, *White Buildings* in 1926. Son of a middle-western business man, he was saturated in Rimbaud and his theory of forcing the body to extremes of consciousness. Homosexual and alcoholic, Crane's existence grew increasingly precarious and violent down to his suicide from a liner when returning from Cuba in 1932. He also acknowledges Whitman. *The Bridge* (Brooklyn Bridge) is his attempt at a 'Song of America', the lyrics, strung together, are deliberately overstrained in the manner of *Bateau ivre*. Several of them, however, are near-perfect and the whole allegory a masterpiece of neo-romanticism. *The Bridge* was subsidised by Otto Kahn, and at the end of his short life

Crane was writing a series of delicate exotics to be called *Key West*. . . .

'The tarantula rattling at the lily's foot . . .'

65 T. S. ELIOT (1888-1965)
ASH WEDNESDAY (1929)

The poems were originally each headed (in Leonard Woolf's copy) by a quotation from the Arnaut Daniel passage in *The Inferno*. They represent the first fruits of Eliot's conversion (1927) after the despair of 'The Hollow Men', and are among his most beautiful lyrics. In one sense Eliot turned against modernism and in 'After Strange Gods' he refers to our world as 'worm-eaten with liberalism', but as a poet he never forsook the revolutionary conception of the melodic line and musical structure of a poem which distinguishes his work from the static metres of, for example, de la Mare and Graves. 'A thin firm minor music of ceremonious intricacy; a religious poem which contains no slovenly phrase, no borrowed zeal, no formulated piety' (Kenner).

66 EZRA POUND (b. 1885)
THIRTY CANTOS
(1930, Paris; 1933, London)

These Cantos, the first half of which were published in 1925, represent the best work in Pound's 'poem of some length' which is still in progress. There are more lyrics and fewer chunks of prose than in the later, not so many economic propositions and ideograms, and some beautiful passages on the Homeric world and renaissance Italy. I prefer them to all the rest except for some passages in the *Pisan Cantos*. The actual texture of the Cantos is for the most part poetical. One enters them like a sunlit church with a service going on in a dark corner and suddenly the music pierces:

> 'There is a wine-red glow in the shallows
> A tin flash in the sun-dazzle. . . .'

A moment later all is muttering and mumbling.

67 EDITH SITWELL (1887-1964)

COLLECTED POEMS

(1930, London and New York)

> 'Beneath those laden boughs' the gardener sighs,
> 'Dreaming in endlessness, forgotten beauty lies.'

This book is a beautiful object in itself and includes her selection from earlier volumes—*Façade* (1922), *Bucolic Comedies* (1923), *Sleeping Beauty* (1924), *Troy Park* (1925), *Elegy on Dead Fashions* (1926) and *Gold Coast Customs* (1929) which Yeats so admired, with an additional ending. The baroque dreamland of the *Sleeping Beauty*, the savage rhythms of *Gold Coast Customs*, the effervescence of *Façade* all belie her statement that 'technique is a matter of physique—since *Goblin Market* there has been no technically sufficient poem written by a woman'.

'It is very strange that you should have said what you did about Ravel and *The Sleeping Beauty*; for various works of Ravel were running through my head, continuously, at the time I was writing it, I am particularly happy that you like that poem . . . (from a letter).

PART III

1930-1940

THE 'THIRTIES

THE disastrous decade. Infiltration of literature by destructive influences of Surrealism (sacrifice of critical standards to auto-intoxication) and politics (exhaustion of talent in lost causes like anti-fascism, popular fronts, etc.). Increasing isolation and smugness of the non-political, increasing anger and controversy, frustration and anxiety culminating in war. Exceptions: some lonely figures liberated by the new fraternal feelings, some poets given new themes; expatriates, driven home by slump, develop social consciences. Nevertheless a good period to be young in, especially during the first years of hope with the world still keeping open for the traveller (Bali, Afghanistan, etc.). The modern impetus far from exhausted. One notices its nihilistic aspect flaring up in Céline, Henry Miller and in the spread of American gangster novels (Dashiel Hammett, Greene's *Brighton Rock*), and the revolutionary logic developing in Aragon, Eluard and early Spender, Day Lewis and Auden: Cummings translates Aragon's banned political poem (*Front Rouge*). Spender collaborates with Eluard in poems of the Spanish war, Malraux writes his novels of political action. Towards the end Orwell and Koestler enter the scene. The aesthetic qualities and technical experiments typical of the Movement are confined to older writers, to Joyce and his contemporary Virginia Woolf (both 1881-1941) and to the group round *transition*. Auden is however by far the most naturally gifted poet since Eliot (who now concentrates on criticism and verse drama) and he writes with energetic facility in many forms. Dylan Thomas is the only successful anglo-surrealist. Michaux and Queneau emerge in France as experimental writers and Sartre on the more conventional left wing. The decade, in America, of Frost and Faulkner, Stevens and Williams, with Cummings silting up. Pound is head-deep in polemics; Wyndham Lewis becomes a fascist; Joyce an eikon; Yeats an angry old man. Gide and Valéry are no longer the gods they were in the 'twenties. One might say that for the first time the new intake is not of the same quality as the generation of Lawrence (1885), Eliot (1888), whom they will replace. There is a dearth of oxygen but far more constructive thinking came forth than in the 'twenties, especially in New York and Paris, though fewer works of art. There is more here for the sociologist and the historian of the human spirit than for James' the 'lonely old artist man'.

---

68 ANTOINE DE SAINT EXUPÉRY
(1900-1945)
VOL DE NUIT (1931)

Translated *Night Flight* by Stuart Gilbert. One of the first and best novels of action or rather a prose poem in which the mystique of the airman makes its appearance. Subsequent books confirmed that the aristocratic humanist Saint Exupéry (1900-44) was indeed a born writer. *Night Flight*, an austere study of the granite-hearted controller of night couriers, was introduced by André Gide, and an immediate success. His best book was *Terre des Hommes* (1939), a new vision of the earth formed by flying (translated as *Wind, Sand and Stars* by Lewis Galantière); he disappeared shot down on a mission near Corsica in the summer of 1944.

– 69 WILLIAM FAULKNER (1897-1962)

SANCTUARY

(1931, New York)

Critics enthuse on *The Sound and the Fury* (1929), or prefer one of the long southern novels like *Light in August*, or *Absalom, Absalom*. *Sanctuary*, however, was written in haste when Faulkner was tired of never selling; like the stories in *These Thirteen* (same year), it is Faulkner for the non-Faulknerites, determined to shock. The adventures of the debutante Temple Drake with her impotent gangster-lover, Pop-eye, who kidnaps her from parents and fiancé, remind one of Don Giovanni. It has been suggested that the enormous appeal of the underworld is that it contains the true vitality of America in its code. It is the world of the subconscious and the Id with the police and law as super ego. Pop-eye is Pluto, according to this myth, who abducts Temple Drake to be his murky queen. The novel was a popular success though attacked by Wyndham Lewis in his *Men Without Art* and I offer it here with an apology for not liking Faulkner better.

70 VIRGINIA WOOLF (1882-1941)

THE WAVES (1931)

Her most experimental novel in which a group of 'early Bloomsburies' with qualities amalgamated from Keynes, Strachey, Vanessa Bell and Desmond McCarthy, etc., are halted in a series of close-ups at various stages of their lives while their thought-trains are recorded, till they end in a crescendo of highly artificial writing that surprisingly comes off. She has described in her diary the agony, the manic exaltation which came over her as she completed the last pages of Bernard's revery.

'Saturday, February 7th.

'Here in the few minutes that remain, I must record, heaven be praised, the end of *The Waves*. I wrote the words O Death fifteen minutes ago, having reeled across the last ten pages with some moments of such intensity and intoxication that I seemed only to stumble after my own voice, or almost after some sort of speaker (as when I was mad). I was almost afraid, remembering the voices that used to fly ahead.'

The novel is 'timed' by a corresponding sequence of seascapes at different hours of the day (a device suggesting Debussy's *La Mer* of which Satie said 'I like best the part around quarter past eleven'). These prose-poems are a little too contrived and somewhat overbalance this, her most ambitious novel.

71 EDMUND WILSON (b. 1895)

AXEL'S CASTLE

(1931, New York and London)

Most of Wilson's critical writing consists of reprinted reviews. *To the Finland Station* (1940) is excluded from this list, alas, as historical. In *Axel's Castle* he developed a Marxist critique of several of our key writers (Yeats, Valéry, Eliot, Proust, Joyce, Stein, Villiers and Rimbaud) and so inaugurated the Marxist onslaught of the 'thirties. Wilson, however, was too perceptive, too much of an artist, not to adore what he was burning—these writers who carried the exploration of the individual to a point from which it could not be taken further. Some of them were rehabilitated in the next decade by Sir Maurice Bowra in his *Heritage of Symbolism* (1943) and *Creative Experiment* (1949); Axel's world of the private imagination in isolation from the life of society does seem however to have been developed as far as possible this side of insanity. The book ends with a capital and little known account of the Dada movement by Tristan Tzara.

72 T. S. ELIOT (1888-1965)
SELECTED ESSAYS (1932)

Eliot's first impact as a critic came with *The Sacred Wood* in 1920. Many pieces from it are reprinted in this volume together with further studies of the Elizabethans, Dante, Baudelaire, etc., sufficient to make this the most important critical work of its kind (for *The Sacred Wood* took a long time to circulate). The essays 'Tradition and the Individual Talent' (1917) and 'The Function of Criticism' (1923) are central to the new criticism. Some criticism affects writers, some readers, some other critics: Eliot's here is of the first kind and administers several oblique *coups de grâce*. He did not so much advance obscure writers or air revolutionary views as apply his severe philosophical training to removing the varnish, like a picture restorer. from accepted masters sheltering behind the cult of personality in their costly frames.

73 W. H. AUDEN (b. 1907)
THE ORATORS (1932)

More influential and characteristic than his *Poems* (1930 and 1933). Although Auden considers *The Orators* a failure and it is sometimes difficult to know where parody leaves off and poetry begins, and although this poetry is uneven, there has been nothing like *The Orators* before or since, and it introduces the whole cast of the 'thirties ('Stephen', 'Christopher',

'Rex') in a series of arcane but belligerent prose poems in which the airman mystique predominates. Dedicated unforgettably to Stephen Spender

> 'Private faces in public places
> are wiser and kinder
> than public faces in private places.'

– 74 LOUIS-FERDINAND CÉLINE
(1894-1961)
VOYAGE AU BOUT DE LA NUIT
(1932, Paris)

Translated by John Marks as *Journey to the End of Night.* Céline (real name Destouches) was wounded and trepanned, afterwards becoming a naval doctor who travelled widely. Anti-war and anti-semitic, he fell foul of both allies and Germans and died miserably in Denmark. As a doctor in a Paris suburb, he wrote his long despairing novel about the squalor of petty bourgeois humanity in the industrial age in a picaresque colloquial style which had an immediate influence on Henry Miller (*Tropic of Cancer*, 1934), and Orwell (*Down and Out in Paris and London*, 1935)—and finally Henry Green. He followed it up with his still gloomier *Mort à Credit* (*Death on the Instalment Plan*, 1938) in which his anti-semiticism came out. When his first novel was published he was working without a salary at a working man's clinic in Clichy. His first book is his most original. The hero, Bardamu, is an anarchical, Rabelaisian, much-travelled doctor like himself, with a gift of invective and a compassion for the underdog.

75 ALDOUS HUXLEY (1894-1963)
BRAVE NEW WORLD (1932)

When, in a Lawrence novel, a dynamic little man with a red or black beard begins to hold forth to admiring women on the world's need for leadership, one feels as if a very noisy street-drill has begun again. In Huxley's novels from *Antic Hay* onwards a similar donkey-engine is untiringly at work. (Lawrence himself is described as Rampion in *Point Counterpoint* and sermonises for both.) In *Brave New World* Huxley subdues the noise of the engine to the brilliantly plausible fantasy he has constructed from his scientific gleanings. (Compare his anthology, *Texts and Pretexts* for the same year.) It is a Utopia which is never dull, of which the horror is always credible as one's sympathies grow more involved with the fate of the young primitive from the Indian Reservation who challenges the machine. This sparkle is absent from *Point Counterpoint* and *Eyeless in Gaza* but returns for the best part of his later mystical novel, *Time must have a Stop*.

76 NATHANAEL WEST (1902-1940)
MISS LONELYHEARTS (1933)

Another horror-comic—but here the horror is in the exploitation of emotion by modern methods of publicity (Miss Lonelyhearts is a young man who edits a gossip column and is driven to despair through getting involved with his readers' problems). West (whose real name was Nathan Weinstein) graduated through Surrealism as an expatriate and afterwards wrote an excellent novel about Hollywood, *The Day of the Locust*. He was killed in a motor accident aged thirty-seven. *Miss Lonelyhearts* was described by an American critic as 'one of the masterpieces of modern literature' for its 'formal perfection, spareness and clarity of style, the tight coherence of its conception'. Stanley Hyman writes: '*Miss Lonelyhearts* seems to me one of the three finest novels of our century. The other two are Scott Fitzgerald's *The Great Gatsby* and Ernest Hemingway's *The Sun also Rises*. It is as fitting an epitome of the 'thirties as they are of the 'twenties. It stands at the end of the line.'

77 ANDRÉ MALRAUX (b. 1895)
LA CONDITION HUMAINE (1933)

Translated *Man's Fate* by Haakon Chevalier and *Storm in Shanghai* by Alastair Macdonald (Methuen, 1934). Malraux began as an orientalist and was in charge of a successful archaeological mission to Cambodia (*The Royal Road*) in 1923. He belonged to the Kuomintang till 1927 and became Associate Secretary General, a member of the Committee of Twelve with Chiang Kai-Shek in a coalition with the Communists, finally propaganda commissioner. His great novel which also brought him fame combines his new philosophy of action with a deep knowledge of the East and culminates in the unforgettable scenes of herosim under torture when Chiang liquidated the Communists. The novel set the pace for many books on the courage and fortitude of left-wing heroes under duress, none of which were as effective because, as Jaloux wrote, Malraux's hero is one who seeks adventure 'not for its own sake but to discover his true nature'—for this reason he is obsessed, as were so many other writers to be, with torture and what it might do to him.

78 DYLAN THOMAS (1914-1953)
(a) *18 POEMS* (1934)
(b) *TWENTY-FIVE POEMS* (1936)

'The force that through the green fuse drives the flower' (included in *Collected Poems*, 1953). Dylan Thomas came poetically of age with two other poets—David Gascoyne and George Barker, all chosen by David Archer for the Parton Press. These first poems (very uneven) shattered for those who discovered them the whole revolutionary optimism of the 'thirties. 'I see the boys of summer in their ruin' cancelled out 'O Comrades, o young comrades' of Spender and restored mystery to verse. The difficult but rewarding crypto-christian sonnet sequence of *Twenty-Five Poems* (another unprocurable) led on to an ambiguous period, when Thomas wrote for little magazines and re-shaped his poems to suit the surrealist canon. This stage culimnated in *The Map of Love* (1939), which also included his early stories.

79 SCOTT FITZGERALD (1896-1940)
– *TENDER IS THE NIGHT* (1934)

This novel is over-praised. Fitzgerald wrote the last part in a great hurry and some of it when drunk so that it becomes little more than an undigested diary. The beginning however is a wonderful evocation of the second phase of American expatriates ensconced in glittering villas on the Riviera in contrast to the home-spun tipplers of *The Sun Also Rises*. The break-down of a marriage in which the doctor-husband, having fulfilled his healing role, makes it inevitable that his wife should leave him, is described with flashes of genius by an expert in self-destruction, and there is a haunting account of Fitzgerald's own pet drunk, the story-teller Ring Lardner (Abe North) and of the predicament of 'grace under pressure' from too many parties and too much money.

80 HENRY JAMES (1843-1916)

THE ART OF THE NOVEL

(1934, New York)

With an introduction by R. P. Blakmur. These eighteen prefaces to the twenty-four volumes of the *Collected Works* (1908, New York) represent the masterpiece of James' criticism, crest of the great wave of Jamesian studies that have continued ever since. 'These notes', he wrote, 'represent, over a considerable course, the continuity of an artist's endeavour, the growth of his whole operative consciousness.'—'To criticise', he wrote in the preface to *What Maisie Knew*, 'is to appreciate, to appropriate, to take intellectual possession.' Also memorable for its snatches of biography, its glimpses of Paris hotels, Venetian palaces, dinner-table conversations where the chance word is dropped, the '*donnée*' round which the next pearl is accreted.

81 MARIANNE MOORE (b. 1887)

SELECTED POEMS

(1935, New York and London)

Miss Moore is a contemporary of Edith Sitwell and her friend Eliot wrote an introduction to this selection and arranged the order. She had been poetry editor of the *Dial* and with Eliot and Cummings had received the Dial Award (1922, 1924, 1925). She has a very precise and original mind (another harpsichord player) and builds the most elaborate mental constructions round unusual facts of natural history. She is more precise and cerebral than Dame Edith. In the pharmacology of the Modern Movement she occupies the place of an imperceptible vitamin of little-known properties whose absence could prove terminal. Her best known poem 'The Pangolin', appeared just after this selection, which includes 'The Octopus', 'Marriage', 'The Jerboa'. 'Only the pedantic literalist could consider the subject-matter to be trivial' (T. S. Eliot). 'My poetry is an imaginary garden full of real toads.'

– 82 HENRI DE MONTHERLANT
(b. 1896)
LES JEUNES FILLES (1936-1939)

Four volumes translated and published here in two volumes, *Pity for Women* and *The Lepers* (translated by John Rodker 1937 and 1940). These four brilliant novels in which the narrator is a typical cad-artist of the between-war vintage, are written in Montherlant's pellucid and crisp style and provoked some strong feminine reactions, culminating in Simone de Beauvoir's *Deuxième Sexe*. Montherlant is connected with old families in Catalonia and the Camargue, was wounded in the first war, suspect in the second; his best early novel, *Les Célibataires* (1934). In youth a celebrator of the virtues of bull-fighting, travel, and athletics, Montherlant in his middle period (of these novels) shows great dash though he was soon to adopt the neo-paganism of the Nazis. Costals, the seducer, who defends male energy and inspiration from the debilitating attacks of marriage-minded young girls and their mothers, is typical of the affluent non-poetical Parisian-Bel Ami brought up to date. Yet he is more, for he is a dedicated and antisocial writer, concerned above all with preserving his freedom and lucidity from two women, the blue-stocking pen-pal Andrée Hacquebaut and the bourgeois sex-kitten, young, beautiful, well-to-do Solange Dandillot who represents the greater danger. An Arab mistress and flight to North Africa provide a sentimental solution. All this seems pure Hemingway, but Montherlant himself is greater than Costals, a poet and moralist in his own right, and it is he who directs the drama.

83 HENRI MICHAUX (b. 1899)

(*a*) *VOYAGE EN GRANDE GARABAGNE*

(1936; included in *Ailleurs*, 1948)

(*b*) *AU PAYS DE LA MAGIE*

(1941; included in *Ailleurs*)

Michaux is a Belgian near-surrealist (born in Namur) who ran away to sea, drove a Paris taxi in 1924, visited Chandernagore and took up with the Surrealists. He was influenced by Swift and Kafka and in 1936 produced his first imaginary travel book, followed by the even more extraordinary *Au pays de la Magie* (translated by Richard Ellman, 1941, New Directions). He wrote some fine war poems (*Exorcismes*) and lately has taken to painting and drug-investigation (mescalin). His two imaginary travel books contain flashes of inspired ferocity; the impossible is taken for granted, the inhabitants are detestable but swim in poetry, the fantastic prose-poems seem carved in rock crystal. Our basest impulses are converted to solid fantasy, our nightmares proliferate in the serum of hate. One of the most original writers alive.

– 84 J.-P. SARTRE (b. 1905)
LA NAUSÉE (1938)

Translated as *Nausea* by Robert Baldick (Penguin 1965). Educated at the École Normale and professor at Le Havre, in this year (1938) Sartre emerged from his philosophical studies and produced a metaphysical novel in diary form as well as the stories published in *Le Mur* (1939). The most intelligent novelist since Aldous Huxley, he was soon too influenced by existentialism and also by the Marxist attitude to literature to believe wholly in the work of art; his mind was set to work for ulterior causes. But the seedy rain-swept Bouville (Le Havre) where Roquentin keeps his gloomy diary and pursues his ineffectual historical researches is unforgettable, like the strange phenomenon—half hope, half weakness—which comes over him when he plays *Some of these Days*. . . . What a relief to get back to someone so aware of the queasiness of solitude—to such an original writer with so clear a mind. Sartre's heyday as existentialist chief came in the 'forties but his greatest work, *L'Etre et le Néant* (1943), must be excluded as philosophy. *Huis Clos* is brilliant but too *guignol*, the novels too propagandist, the essays too polemical—except the great texts on Baudelaire, Genet and 'What is Literature?'.

85 LOUIS MACNEICE (1907-1963)
AUTUMN JOURNAL (1939)

'Close and slow, summer is ending in Hampshire.' There are some good poems (e.g. 'Bagpipe Music') in his second book *The Earth Compels* (1938) and in his three war books, *Plant and Phantom*, *Springboard* and *Holes in the Sky*, but even in these one feels that, though immensely gifted and prolific, he is never fully extended, preferring to play a few difficult shots, pick up his glass, and walk away from the table. In *Autumn Journal*, his only long poem, he completely seizes the atmosphere of the year of Munich, he tolls the knell of the political 'thirties with melancholy triumph. Some passages are mere journalism; the needle scratches, but the metre and the variability he lends to it come to his rescue. How different from the casual exhibitionism of *Letters from Iceland* written with Auden at his most ebullient only two years before.

86 CHRISTOPHER ISHERWOOD
(b. 1904)
GOODBYE TO BERLIN (1939)

'I am a camera with its shutter open, quite passive, recording not thinking.' A good year for Isherwood who also collaborated with Auden in *Journey to a War* (1939). His 'Annus Mirabilis' was 1935 with *Mr Norris changes Trains* and his autobiography, *Lions and Shadows*. A serene Marxist who later gravitated into the Vedanta movement round Heard and Huxley, and the most gifted novelist since Greene and Waugh (he is only a year younger), his is an unexpected weakness, a desire to please amounting to ingratiation. There is too much nougat in his early books except for his remarkable novel, *The Memorial*. Berlin under the emergent Nazis provided a stiffening of tragedy here shown in his moving story 'The Nowaks', in the two remarkable Berlin diaries, with Sally Bowles' for comic relief.

87 JAMES JOYCE (1882-1941)
FINNEGANS WAKE (1939)

'A way alone aloved alost along the. . . .' If *Finnegans Wake* is a key book, it is a key which needs a key (*A Skeleton Key to Finnegans Wake* by Campbell was published in 1957). It came out at a bad moment and the mass of critical exercises for which its material is heaven-sent only began to appear as American theses after the war. Nevertheless 'Anna Livia' and other fragments which had been circulating in little magazines and slim volumes since 1925 had an undoubted influence on 'The Revolution of the Word', a revolution in which only writers with private means could enrol. The 'Wake' reminds me of the unfinished obelisk which lies on its side at Assuan, yet it has passages of unearthly beauty (particularly the last page) and huge comic scenes. Joyce insisted that each word, each sentence had several meanings and that the '*idéal lecteur*' should devote his life-time to it, like the Koran. In spite of its random melodies and inspissated felicities it somehow belongs to the passing of the Modern Movement, and fails to communicate its grandeur of conception. The best way to come to it is through the 'Anna Livia' recording and the 'Tales told of Shem and Shaun'.

– 88 GRAHAM GREENE (b. 1904)
THE POWER AND THE GLORY (1940)

Graham Greene is one of the few Catholic writers who is also a modernist. His *Brighton Rock* (1938) in one sense a Catholic novel, is also one of the first gangster stories to depict the vicious fly-blown atmosphere of a typical English seaside resort in the 'thirties. *The Power and the Glory* is about a 'whisky priest' in an anti-Catholic central American country who has forfeited everything but the inalienable power through which he ultimately wins redemption.

Apart from Hopkins, Catholic writers are seldom experimental. Claudel hammers the heretic, ranges himself against Gide, Maritain is all for order and nearly enrols Cocteau who escapes him to be chastized by the Racinian Mauriac. Greene, though conventional in technique, does take his theology into some dark corners and sometimes appears politically, even doctrinally intransigent.

PART IV

1940-1950

THE 'FORTIES

THE 'thirties ended in a blaze of nostalgia, with Joyce's *Finnegans Wake*, Gide's *Journal* covering fifty years, Breton's retrospective *Anthologie de l'Humour Noir*. Thus opened the frustrated 'forties, five years of total war and five more of recrimination and exhaustion during which the Modern Movement unobtrusively expired. Surrealism gave way to Existentialism, the 'new criticism' flourished, Sartre edited Baudelaire's journals and Queneau recast *Bouvard et Pécuchet*. 'In my end is my beginning'; Queneau's *Exercises de Style* (1946) reduced the concept of literature to classified bathos. Breton, Bataille, Genet, Paulhan, Ponge and Michaux continued to experiment but Paris ceased to be the capital of the *avant garde*. The deaths of Yeats, Joyce, Virginia Woolf and Freud were followed by those of Valery and Orwell, Dylan Thomas and Gide.

Why did the Movement peter out? Too many defectors in the Movement itself? Thus while Joyce, Gide, Valéry, Forster ('What I believe', 1939) and Cummings remained humanists of one kind or other to the end, too many seceded; some followed Huysmans into the religious fold (Eliot, Edith Sitwell, Waugh, Auden*), some became fascists (Pound, Lewis), others communists (Eluard, Aragon), others adopted an oriental religion (Huxley). Sartre went Marxist and quarrelled with Camus. Malraux became a politician—he who had introduced in *La Condition Humaine* that literature of the condemned cell which was to produce such fine and char-

* 'We cannot, in literature any more than the rest of life, live in a perpetual state of revolution'.—T. S. Eliot

acteristic work in the 'forties—*For Whom the Bell Tolls*, *Darkness at Noon*, Sartre's *Le Mur* and *Huis Clos*, Camus's *L'Etranger* and *La Peste* and Orwell's *1984*. Perhaps the spirit of the Modern Movement persists today most strongly in the theatre (Artaud, Ionesco, Pinter) where there have been more conventions to overthrow. The recent publication of *Lolita*, *Lady Chatterley* and *Tropic of Cancer* has ended the battle with the censorship which began with the prosecutions of *Les Fleurs du Mal* and *Madame Bovary* more than a century ago. Genet's homosexual rhapsody, *Notre Dame des Fleurs* (1948) carries the victory one stage further.

In 1961 I find the first epitaph—'Robert Graves and the decay of Modernism' as a title by D. J. Enright, while Spender has already been lecturing on them in the past tense (published as *The Struggle of the Moderns*, London, 1964) and the new poets from Larkin onwards are in arms against both the intellectualism of Eliot, and the emotionalism of Thomas. Professor Harry Levin, I am just informed, has delivered a Lecture on 'What was Modernism?'. Yet the twin features of the Movement; faith in the intellect as destroyer of pretences and illusions, as man's true guide wherever it may lead, and the equally strong belief in the validity of the imagination, the enlargement of sensibility, the Côté Voltaire and the Côté Rousseau, or Stendhal and Chateaubriand, must surely continue to inspire a masterpiece, as in the days of Baudelaire, Rimbaud and Proust. For students who are growing up under new tyrannies and new orthodoxies such a list may prove more than a parlour game—a roll of honour; a prisoner's smuggled file; a home.

89 ARTHUR KOESTLER (b. 1905)
DARKNESS AT NOON (1940)

Translated by Daphne Hardy. Another classic of the literature of the condemned cell. Koestler in *Spanish Testament* (Dialogue with Death) had already challenged death to a first duel based on his own experience in Franco's prisons. This time he applied the dialogue to the Russian trials. He knew both Bukharin and Radek and swung the uncommitted Left with him. The book had a considerable influence in France as *Le Zéro et l'Infini* (see Gide's later *Journal*). Unlike Malraux, Koestler has a vein of whimsical Central European humour and lacks combat experience, but gains by his understanding of the psychology of revolution and the propaganda machine.

90 W. H. AUDEN (b. 1907)
ANOTHER TIME

(1940, New York and London. Collected Shorter Poems, 1950)

It is sometimes said of Auden that he has never written a great book but this is certainly his best collection of poems and includes his elegies on Yeats and Freud and everything from 'Lay your sleeping head' and 'About suffering the old masters were never wrong' down to

> 'a crack in the teacup opens
> a lane to the land of the dead. . . .'

and 'we must love one another or die'. This was his first book to be published in America prior to London and was followed by the long metaphysical poem *New Year Letter* in which his conversion is imminent. It is the last Auden, I think, which people learnt by heart, even as Auden was for many of us the last poet we learnt by heart, a continuous exciting effervescence through fifteen years of our lives from his *Poems 1930* to *The Sea and the Mirror*. 'It is right that there should be a young poet who has made himself into a kind of unofficial poet laureate. If I am bombed I hope he will write a few sapphics about me.' (Spender, reviewing this volume).

91 STEPHEN SPENDER (b. 1909)
RUINS AND VISIONS (1942)

'You must live through the time when everything hurts.' Spender's early poetry was characterised by an inspired innocence, he was the type that Lewis christened 'the Revolutionary Simpleton' but it soon became apparent that he had a mind which was independently at work, and his poems on the Spanish war in *The Still Centre* (1939) are far removed from his Communist enthusiasm of 1933. In *Ruins and Visions* his poetry is profoundly affected by the break-up of his marriage and the death of his sister. He has written some of the best poems of despairing grief and separation. The book ends with some charming love poems as he meets his second wife which give the whole work a shape; the visions follow the ruin, instead of announcing it.

As a critic, as a writer of short stories, and through his autobiography, *World within World* which comes just too late for us (1951) Spender belongs deeply to the Movement, bringing to it his own German sources, the influences of Mann, Rilke, Kafka, Hölderlin. His autobiography also includes portraits of Yeats, Edith Sitwell and Virginia Woolf besides his experiences in Berlin and the Spanish war. I should like to have included his early poems; there is something quite new and strange about them but too many grow dense and curdle.

– 92 T. S. ELIOT (1888-1965)
FOUR QUARTETS
(1943-1944, New York and London)

The *Four Quartets*, the most important poem since Yeats' *The Tower*, and, as many think, of the century, were written over ten years ('Burnt Norton' in *Collected Poems*, 1935, 'East Coker', 1940; New York publication of *Quartets*, 1943, London, 1944). Although Eliot had long taken leave of modernism as a creed, and disapproved of poetry as a substitute for religion, he had retained the modern advances in technique evolved by him and Pound and the *Quartets* preserve the melodic line, the intricacy of thought and shape which is the high point of his technique applied to what are really religious and philosophical meditations. 'Little Gitting' evokes a seventeenth-century religious community, the 'Dry Salvages' the sea (rocks off Gloucester). The Quartets indicated are late Beethoven and each has four 'movements'. 'Personally I like each one better than its predecessor and Little Gidding best of all. I may be very conceited, but Little Gidding strikes me as one of the best patriotic poems in the language and I think goes a good deal deeper than Tennyson on the *Revenge* or even Walt Whitman' (T. S. Eliot in a letter).

– 93 GEORGE ORWELL (1903-1950)
ANIMAL FARM (1945)

Orwell's first batch of novels were fairly conventional. His *Down and Out in Paris and London* was in the vein of Céline and Miller. The *Road to Wigan Pier* and the much better *Homage to Catalonia* were too full of political argument and statistics. *Animal Farm*, which owes something to Swift and

Defoe, is his masterpiece, the best fable in the language with Boxer the cart-horse, the pigs and the donkey becoming household words. 'What I have most wanted to do throughout the last ten years is to make political writing into an art. . . . *Animal Farm* was the first book in which I tried, with full consciousness of what I was doing, to fuse political purpose and artistic purpose into one whole.'

94 ALBERT CAMUS (1913-1960)
L'ÉTRANGER (1941)

(Translated by Stuart Gilbert, *The Outsider*, 1946)

95 ALBERT CAMUS
LA PESTE (1947)

(Translated by Stuart Gilbert, *The Plague*)

Camus was born at Mondovi, Algeria, of working-class parents. He was actor, playwright, journalist before taking a prominent part in the Resistance and editing *Combat*. He developed his own brand of existentialism which preceded Sartre (*L'Etre et le Néant*, 1943) who afterwards disclaimed him. Camus's brand is explained in *Le Mythe de Sisyphe* (1942) and his play *Caligula*. ('There's only one serious philosophical problem: suicide.') Granted the deceptive illusory quality of life, its logical absurdity, the only free choice is to leave it. But suicide also is absurd. There remains resignation or rebellion. 'I draw three consequences from the Absurdity of things—my rebellion, my freedom and my passion.'

His first novel, *L'Etranger*, is the offspring of this philosophy. The 'outsider' or 'foreigner',

> I, a stranger and afraid
> In a world I never made,

is outside the normal bourgeois rules and framework, cool, unthinking, emotionally under-endowed. He behaves incorrectly at his mother's funeral, murders an Arab in a moment of heat-wave black-out on the beach, is tried and sentenced, feeling all the time as if he were someone else—but Meursault is far from stupid, he is no amoral monster but glides to his doom judging his judges with increasing eloquence. The short novel is written with compelling force and charm, in prose as staccato as a cicada.

La Peste is more ambitious. The years of clandestine activity and commitment to the struggle and handling of men have carried the gentle Camus onward even as Sartre, or as Hemingway changed from *The Sun Also Rises* to *For Whom the Bell Tolls*. *La Peste* represents the liberation of Camus from existentialism into something nearer the collective revolutionary heroism of *La Condition Humaine*. It is an allegory of the German Occupation, transposed as an outbreak of the plague in Oran. The city, townsfolk and epidemic form a single unit in which a 'resistance' group operates, a doctor, a priest, an honourable man of good will. Camus's love and respect for the individual combine with his ironical detachment to generate a claustrophilia so that we are loth to leave the plague-stricken city. After being awarded the Nobel Prize, Camus was killed in a motor accident in 1960.

96 DYLAN THOMAS (1914-1953)
DEATHS AND ENTRANCES
(1946, London; *New Poems*, U.S.A.)

'On almost the incendiary eve.' . . . *Deaths and Entrances* is to be preferred to the American *New Poems* which does not include 'Fern Hill'. The little square book contains some of the best war poetry (from the home front) and Thomas's incantatory descriptions of his childhood. His romantic, regional and religious standpoint is here combined with his surrealist manipulation of language to produce his greatest work. This art (owing something to Crane) was like Crane's, elaborately self-conscious, and trod a tight-rope between rhetoric and sentimentality. It marks the end of Thomas's inspiration, except for half a dozen poems in the next few years which appeared in *In Country Sleep*, New York, and *Collected Poems*, 1952—the last port of call before we embark upon a sea of legend.

97 JOHN BETJEMAN (b. 1906)
SELECTED POEMS
(1948, London)

This selection was made and introduced by the anti-modernist John Sparrow. Is Betjeman a modernist at all, any more than Housman or Emily Dickinson? His versification is traditional, steeped in Tennysonian rhythms, Hymns A. and M., Cowper, Hardy; but his sensibility—that surely belongs to this age. It is deep, discriminating, perverted and unique. It is not merely his nostalgia for the past, it is the bifocal self-consciousness of it, found also in his sense of place and views on sex. Like Auden, he is a poet whom one learns by heart, or like Tennyson, rather, one who slides by bits and pieces into the common experience of the race. The chain of small explosions detonated by his slim volumes from *Mount Zion* (1931), are individually too insignificant to demand separate notice but the Warden of All Souls has made a cumulative selection from them. Even so some of his best poems are found in *A few late Chrysanthemums* which came out the following year.

98 EZRA POUND (b. 1885)

THE PISAN CANTOS

(1948, New York; 1949, London)

The Pisan Cantos were roughly drafted when Pound was imprisoned by the American army authorities in a camp at Pisa and were published when he was an inmate of St Elizabeth's Hospital in Washington in 1948. He presumably had no access to his books when they were written. The eleven cantos in fact, form an autobiography, the main theme being the memories of his youth in Venice and England (1908-14) put together by 'Odysseus' Pound on his storm-tossed raft. He does not abandon his economic prejudices or his Confucian sanity; he accepts his prison camp with resignation but for the first time, he experiences remorse and the '*nessun maggior dolore*' of Dante.

> Nothing matters but the quality of the affection—
> in the end—that has carved the trace in the mind
> what thou lovest well is thy true heritage
> what thou lovest well shall not be reft from thee.

The weather in the cantos is like our own; a prevailing south west wind of rainy allusiveness blows most of the time, sometimes turning to a fog of economic prosing, sometimes to an occasional glimpse of radiant Mediterranean sunshine. All are present here, especially nostalgia, often magical. 'Oh let an old man rest.'

99 GEORGE ORWELL (1903-1950)

1984 (1949)

Orwell's commanding influence in the 'forties derived from his essays and journalism (*Inside the Whale*, 1940, and *Critical*

Essays, 1946), but his last novel which appeared a year before his death had the same success (rare for Utopias) as *Brave New World*. 'Dystopias' would be a better word for them. It has been called an embittered book and Winston Smith and his girl friend are inclined to be puppets, but it is written with his particular feeling and clarity and though it flags sometimes with his growing fatigue even the political arguments are never dull. In fact they are worked out with passionate logic. 'Double Think', 'Newspeak', 'Big Brother' now form part of the language. It is a warning against totalitarianism under any disguise—left or right. It is also a warning based on Auden's 'We must love one another or die' for if the lovers had been able to maintain complete trust in each other, even under torture, then only their bodies would have been broken.

100 WILLIAM CARLOS WILLIAMS
(1883-1963)

PATERSON, 1, 2, 3, 4,
(1946-1951, New York; 1964, London)

'No ideas but in things.'

The first four books of *Paterson* were finished by October 1950 and are complete in themselves. Williams has been with us, like Pound and Eliot, throughout the Movement though he regarded Eliot as the betrayer of the revolution by handing power over to academic intellectuals. A hard-working general practitioner, he was born in 1883 in Rutherford, New Jersey (Paterson), and spent most of his life there. Pound introduced him in his imagist anthologies. He went to England and brought out a book there, he studied medicine in Paris, his poems were in all the little magazines. *Paterson* is both a man and a city as Joyce's Earwicker is both a man and a hill. The long poem has many moods and includes quotations from letters by Pound and Ginsberg, large Seurat-like canvases of the Park on Sunday, intimate Bonnard-like interiors, uproarious comedy. The Passaic river becomes to him what the polluted Bièvre was to Huysmans. 'A poem is a complete little universe, it exists separately. Any poem that has worth expresses the whole life of the poet.' 'No ideas but in the facts'—his poem is written with a deep aversion to all forms of pretentiousness, rhetoric or prepared effects; it runs eddying along, broken by old letters, bits of local history and limpid love lyrics. 'Nothing is good', he wrote, 'save the new'—which brings us back to Baudelaire:

'Au fond de l'Inconnu pour trouver du *nouveau*.'

NOTES ON THE BIBLIOGRAPHY

Scope. The bibliography gives details of works included in the numbered sections of the book, omitting those cited only in the introduction.

First Editions. The place, publisher and date of the main work in each section, and the date of any other work by the same author cited in that section are given. Physically distinct editions of a work are separated by a semi-colon, as in (1). The publication of parts of a work before the first edition has not been noted, except in (26), (87) and (92).

Available Texts. In the sections h. and p., the general aim has been to give one hardback and one paperback edition respectively. In some cases, an out-of-print edition, indicated by an asterisk(*), has been included. Dates are only given where they seem especially useful.

Where the work cited is French, another section, f., gives an available French text. Where possible, the inexpensive paperback series *Le livre de poche*, published in Paris, has been cited, with the number in the series of the particular work. The excellent but much more expensive series *Bibliothèque de la Pléiade*, published by *Gallimard*, and often printing the complete works of an author in one or two volumes, is cited only once, but includes, of the writers discussed in this book: Apollinaire; Baudelaire; Camus; Céline; Flaubert; Gide; Mallarmé; Malraux; Montherlant; Proust (*À la recherche du temps perdu* in 3 volumes); Rimbaud; Saint-Éxupery; and Valéry. Two other French series, both quite cheap, might be noted here. *Écrivains de toujours*, published by *Les Éditions du Seuil*, gives a brief illustrated introduction to the life and work of each author, using numerous extracts from his writings; it includes: Apollinaire; Baudelaire; Camus; Cocteau; Flaubert; Gide; Mallarmé; Malraux; Maupassant; Montherlant; Rimbaud; Saint-Éxupery and Sartre. *Poètes d'aujourd'hui* published by *Seghers*, has a long introduction, a selection from the author's works, and a bibliography in each volume; included are: Apollinaire; Baudelaire; Breton; Jarry; Michaux; and Rimbaud.

IMPRINT. In f., it is Paris, unless otherwise stated; in h. and p., it is London, unless otherwise stated. *New Directions* are given as being published in New York, although in some cases Norfolk, Conn., was the original place of publication. *Gallimard* is given in all cases where the work bears the imprint *Éditions de la NRF.*

ABBREVIATIONS

c.	= copyright date	introd.	= introduction by
C.U.P.	= Cambridge University Press	O.U.P.	= Oxford University Press
comp.	= compiled by	p.	= paperback edition
cont.	= contains	pub.	= published
ed.	= edited by	repr.	= reprint, -ed
edn	= edition	rev.	= revised
enl.	= enlarged	trans.	= translated by
Everyman	= Everyman's Library	vol(s)	= volume(s)
		*	= out-of-print
f.	= French text	=	= translated as; published as
h.	= hardback edition		

AMERICAN EDITIONS. For American readers an attempt has been made to list all editions, both hardback and paperback, which are currently available in the United States.

BIBLIOGRAPHY

1 HENRY JAMES *The Portrait of a Lady*. London: Macmillan, 1881; Boston, New York: Houghton, Mifflin, 1881 [given in book as 1882].

=vols. 3-4 of *The Novels and Tales of Henry James*, New York: Scribner, 1908. (New York edition.) [Revised.]

h. introd. Grahame Greene. O.U.P. (World's Classics). [New York edn text.]

p. Penguin. [1881 text.]

American editions

h. Houghton (2 vols.).

h., p. ed. Leon Edel. Houghton (1 vol.); Riverside.

h. =vols. 3-4 of *The Novels of Henry James*. Scribner. (New York Edition.) [Revised.]

h. sels. In: *The Henry James Reader*; ed. Leon Edel. (*Washington Square; The Aspern Papers; Daisy Miller; Pandora* and selections from 20 novels and 120 tales.) Scribner.

h. introd. Grahame Greene. O.U.P. (World's Classics). [New York edn. text.]

p. Collier.

p. introd. R. P. Blackmur. Dell: Laurel.

p. introd. Fred B. Millet. Modern Library; Modern Library College Editions.

p. afterword Oscar Cargill. New American Library: Signet.

p. Penguin.

p. ed. Robert J. Dixson. Regents Pub. Co. [Adapted.]

p. introd. Quentin Anderson. Washington Square Pr.

2 GUSTAVE FLAUBERT *Bouvard et Pécuchet*. Paris: A. Lemerre, 1881.

f. Le livre de poche, 440-441.

h. *Bouvard and Pécuchet*; trans. T. W. Earp and G. W. Stonier. New York: New Directions; Cape.*

Note also:

f. *Dictionnaire des Idées Reçues.* Paris: Nouvel Office d'Édition.

h. =*Dictionary of Accepted Ideas*; trans. Jacques Barzun. Reinhardt.

American edition

h. trans. T. W. Earp & G. W. Stonier; introd. Lionel Trilling. New Directions.

Note also:

h. =*Dictionary of Accepted Ideas*; trans. Jacques Barzun. New Directions.

p. =*Dictionary of Platitudes.* A. S. Barnes: Perpetua Books.

3 VILLIERS DE L'ISLE ADAM *Contes Cruels.* Paris: Calmann-Lévy, 1883.

f. ed. P. G. Castex et J. Bollery. Corti.; Union Générale d'Éditions (10 × 18).

h. =*Cruel Tales*; trans. Robert Baldick. O.U.P.

L'Ève Future, 1886.

f. Pauvert.

h.

Axël, 1890.

f. La Colombe.

h. *Axel*; trans. H. P. R. Finberg, preface by W. B. Yeats. Jarrolds.*

American edition

Contes Cruels.

h. =Cruel Tales; trans. Robert Baldick O.U.P.

4 JORIS KARL HUYSMANS *À Rebours.* Paris: Charpentier, 1884.

f. Fasquelle.

h. =*Against the Grain.* Paris: Groves & Michaux*; Fortune Press.*

p. *Against Nature*; trans. Robert Baldick. Penguin.

American edition

À Rebours.

p. =*Against Nature*; trans. Robert Baldick. Penguin.

5 CHARLES BAUDELAIRE *Oeuvres Posthumes*. Paris: Quantin, 1887.

f. =*Écrits Intimes*; introd. J.-P. Sartre. Paris: Point du jour, 1946.*

=*Journaux Intimes*; *Fusées*; *Mon coeur mis à nu*; *Carnet*; éd. Jacques Crépet et Georges Blin. Paris: Corti, 1949.

h. =*Intimate Journals*; trans. Christopher Isherwood, introd. T. S. Eliot. Blackamore Press, 1930*; introd. W. H. Auden. Methuen, 1949.*

See also: *Baudelaire: A Self Portrait: Selected Letters*; trans. Lois B. & Francis E. Hyslop. O.U.P.*

American edition: none

6 ARTHUR RIMBAUD *Les Illuminations*. Paris: La Vogue, 1886. *Les Illuminations; Une Saison en Enfer*. Paris: Vanier, 1892.

f. In: *Poésies Complètes*. Le livre de poche, 498.

p. =*Illuminations and Other Prose Poems*; trans. Louise Varèse; rev. edn. [Bilingual.] New York: New Directions. *Or*,

In: *Rimbaud*; introd. and ed. Oliver Bernard. [Bilingual.] Penguin.

American editions

p. =*Illuminations*; trans. Louise Varèse. [Bilingual.] New Directions.

p. in *Selected Verse*; ed. Oliver Bernard. Penguin.

h. in *Selected Verse*; trans. Oliver Bernard. Gloucester, Mass.: Peter Smith.

7 STÉPHANE MALLARMÉ *Les Poésies*. Paris: Revue indépendante, 1887.

f. *Poésies Complètes*. Geneva, Cailler.

h. *Poems;* trans. Roger Fry. [Bilingual.] New York: New Directions.

p. In: *Mallarmé:* introd. and ed. Anthony Hartley. [Bilingual]. Penguin.

Henri Mondor, *Vie de Mallarmé*.

f. édn complète. Gallimard.

American editions

h. =*Poems*; trans. Roger Fry. [Bilingual.] New Directions: New Classics.

h., p. *Selected Poems*; trans. C. F. MacIntyre. [Bilingual.] Berkeley: University of California Pr.

8 GUY DE MAUPASSANT *Bel Ami*. Paris: Havard, 1885.

f. Le livre de poche, 619-620.

h. trans. Eric Sutton. Hamish Hamilton.*

p. trans. H. N. P. Sloman. Penguin.

Boule de Suif, 1880. [In the collection: *Les Soirées de Médan*, by Zola, de Maupassant and others.]

La Maison Tellier, 1881.

f. *Contes et Nouvelles*. 3 vols. Michel.
Boule de Suif. Le livre de poche, 650.
La Maison Tellier. Le livre de poche, 760.

h. 88 *Short Stories*. Cassell.
88 *More Stories*. Cassell.

p. *Short Stories*; trans. Marjorie Laurie. Dent (Everyman Paperbacks).
Boule de Suif and Other Stories; trans. H. N. P. Sloman. Penguin.* [Contains *La maison Tellier*.]

American editions

Bel-Ami.

p. trans. H. N. P. Sloman. Penguin.

p. Popular Library.

Boule de Suif.

h. *Best Short Stories*. Modern Library.

h. *Short Stories*. Dutton: Everyman's.

h. *Contes Choisis*; ed. W. R. Price. Odyssey.

h., p. *The Portable Maupassant*; ed. Lewis Galantière. Viking Portable.

p. *Boule de Suif, and Other Stories*; trans H. N. P. Sloman. Penguin.

p. *The Best Short Stories of de Maupassant*; ed. Gerald Hopkins. Premier.

Boule de Suif and Selected Stories; trans. Andrew R. McAndrew; fwd. Edwin D. Sullivan. New American Library: Signet.

p. *Maupassant: A Laurel Reader*; ed. Francis Steegmuller. Dell: Laurel.
p. *Contes Choisis*. (Fr.) Doubleday: Anchor.

9 EDMOND ET JULES DE GONCOURT *Journal*. Paris: Charpentier (Fasquelle), 1887-96.
f. éd. définitive. 4 vols. Fasquelle, Flammarion.
h. =*The Goncourt Journals, 1851-1870*; trans. Lewis Galantière. Cassell, 1937.* [Selection.]
=*Pages from the Goncourt Journal*; trans. Robert Baldick. O.U.P.

American edition
h. =*Pages from the Goncourt Journal*; ed. & trans. Robert Baldick. O.U.P.

10 JORIS KARL HUYSMANS *Là-bas*. Paris: Tresse et Stock, 1891.
f. Le livre de poche, 725.
h. *Down There: A Study of Satanism*; trans. Keene Wallis. New York: University Books.
En Rade, 1887.
f. Plon.*

American edition
h. =*Down There: A Study of Satanism*; trans. Keene Wallis. University Books.

11 ALFRED JARRY *Ubu Roi*. Paris: Mercure de France, 1896.
f. *Tout Ubu*. Le livre de poche, 838-839.
p. trans. Barbara Wright. Gaberbocchus Press.
Ubu Cocu, 1944.
f. In: *Tout Ubu* as above.
h. trans. Cyril Connolly. In: *Selected Works*; ed. Roger Shattuck & Simon Watson Taylor. Methuen, 1965.

American editions
Ubu Roi.
h. =*King Ubu*. In: *Modern French Theatre: An Anthology of Plays*; ed. & trans. Michael Benedikt and George E. Wellwarth. Dutton.

p. =*Ubu Roi*; trans. Barbara Wright. New Directions.
p. =*Ubu Roi*. In: *Four French Comedies*. Putnam: Capricorn.

Ubu Cocu.

h. trans. Cyril Connolly. In: *Selected Works*; ed. Roger Shattuck & Simon Watson Taylor. Grove.

12 HENRY JAMES *The Awkward Age*. London: Heinemann; New York, London: Harper, 1899.

=vol. 9 of *The Novels and Tales of Henry James*, New York: Scribner, 1908. (New York edition.)

h. Hamish Hamilton*; New York: Scribner. [New York Edition text.]

American edition

h. =vol. 9 of *The Novels and Tales of Henry James*. Scribner. (New York Edition.)

13 ANDRÉ GIDE *L'Immoraliste*. Paris: Mercure de France, 1902.

f. Le livre de poche, 372.
h. =*The Immoralist*; trans. Dorothy Bussy. Cassell.
p. as above. Penguin.

Les Nourritures Terrestres, 1897.

f. Gallimard; Le livre de poche, 1258.
h. =*Fruits of the Earth*; trans. Dorothy Bussy. Secker and Warburg.*

American editions

L'Immoraliste.

h., p. =*The Immoralist*. Knopf; Knopf: Vintage.
h., p. =*L'Immoralist*; ed. Elaine Marks & Richard Tedeschi. (Fr.) Macmillan.

14 JOSEPH CONRAD *Youth: A Narrative, and Two Other Stories*. Edinburgh and London; Blackwood, 1902.

h. *Youth, The Heart of Darkness, and The End of the Tether*. Dent.
p. *Three Short Novels* (*Heart of Darkness, Youth, Typhoon*). Harrap (Bantam Library).

American editions

h. *Youth: A Narrative, and Two Other Stories*. Nelson: Nelson Classics.

h., p. *The Portable Conrad*; ed. Morton D. Zabel. Viking; Viking Portable.

p. *Youth, Heart of Darkness, and The End of the Tether*; ed. Morton D. Zabel. Doubleday: Anchor.

p. *Heart of Darkness, Almayer's Folly, and Lagoon*. Dell.

p. *Heart of Darkness and The Secret Sharer*. New American Library: Signet.

p. *Heart of Darkness: With Backgrounds and Criticisms*; ed. Leonard Dean. Prentice-Hall.

15 JOSEPH CONRAD *The Secret Agent*. London: Methuen, 1907.

h. Dent.

p. Penguin; Dent (Everyman Paperbacks).

Nostromo, 1904.

h. Dent. p. Penguin.

T. S. Eliot, *The Hollow Men*.

See 30, 65.

American editions

The Secret Agent.

h. Nelson: Nelson Classics.

p. Doubleday: Anchor.

Nostromo.

h. Modern Library.

p. Dell.

p. ed. Dorothy Van Ghent. Rinehart.

p. New American Library: Signet.

p. Penguin.

16 HENRY JAMES *The Ambassadors*. London: Methuen; New York, London: Harper, 1903.

h. Dent (Everyman). p. Dent (Everyman Paperbacks).

The Sacred Fount, 1901.

h. Introd. Leon Edel. Hart-Davis.

American editions

h. Dutton: Everyman.

h. Harper.

h., p. ed. Leon Edel. Houghton; Houghton: Riverside.
h. Scribner. (2 vols.)
p. Dell.
p. Fawcett: Premier.
p. ed. F. W. Dupee. Rinehart.
p. ed. R. W. Stallman. New American Library: Signet
p. Norton.
p. Washington Square Pr.

17 GEORGE MOORE *Memoirs of My Dead Life*. London: Heinemann, 1906.
h. Heinemann.*
Confessions of a Young Man, 1888.
h. Heinemann.
p. Penguin*; New York. Putnam (Capricorn).
'*Hail and Farewell!*', 3 vols., 1911-14.
h. Heinemann.

American edition
Confessions of a Young Man.
p. Putnam: Capricorn.

18 J. M. SYNGE *The Playboy of the Western World*. Dublin: Maunsel, 1907.
h. ed. T. R. Henn. Methuen.
The Plays and Poems; ed. T. R. Henn. Methuen.
p. *The Playboy of the Western World and Riders to the Sea.* Allen & Unwin (Unwin Books).
Riders to the Sea, 1905 [performed 1904].
h, p. see the collections above.

American editions
The Playboy of the Western World.
h. *Complete Works*. Random House.
p. *Playboy of the Western World and Riders to the Sea.* Barnes & Noble.
p. *Complete Plays*. Knopf: Vintage.
Riders to the Sea.
(see above.)

19 E. M. FORSTER *The Longest Journey*. Edinburgh and London: Blackwood, 1907.
h. introduction by the author. O.U.P. (World's Classics); Arnold.
p. Penguin.
Howard's End, 1910.
h. Arnold. p. Penguin.
G. E. Moore, *Principia Ethica*.
h, p. C.U.P.

American editions
The Longest Journey.
h., p. Knopf; Knopf: Vintage.
Howard's End.
p. Knopf: Vintage.
G. E. Moore, *Principia Ethica*.
h., p. =*Ethics*. O.U.P.: Home University Library.

20 NORMAN DOUGLAS *Siren Land*. London: Dent; New York: Dutton, 1911.
h. *Siren Land and Fountains in the Sand*; new edn. Secker & Warburg.
p. Penguin.*
Fountains in the Sand, 1912.
h. as above. p. Penguin.*
Old Calabria, 1915.
h. Secker. p. Penguin.*
W. Somerset Maugham, *Of Human Bondage*.
h. Heinemann. p. Penguin.
Arnold Bennett, *The Old Wives' Tale*.
h. Dent (Everyman). p. Pan Books.

American editions
Old Calabria.
h. Harcourt.
W. Somerset Maugham, *Of Human Bondage*.
h. Doubleday.
h. Modern Library.
p. Knopf: Vintage.
Arnold Bennett, *The Old Wives' Tale*.

h. Modern Library.
h. Nelson: Nelson Classics.
p. New American Library: Signet.

21 D. H. LAWRENCE *Sons and Lovers*. London: Duckworth, 1913.
h. Heinemann. p. Penguin.
The White Peacock, 1911.
h. Heinemann. p. Penguin.
Love Poems and Others, 1913. *Amores*, 1916.
h. *Complete Poems*. 2 vols.; ed. by V. de Sola Pinto and Warren Roberts. Heinemann, 1964.
p. *Selected Poems*. Penguin.
The Rainbow, 1915.
h. Heinemann. p. Penguin.
Women in Love, 1920.
h. Heinemann. p. Penguin.

American editions

Sons and Lovers.
h. Modern Library.
p. Viking: Compass.
Love Poems and Others; Amores.
h. *The Complete Poems of D. H. Lawrence*; ed. Vivian De Sola Pinto & F. Warren Roberts. Viking.
h., p. *The Portable D. H. Lawrence*; ed. Diana Trilling. Viking Portable.
The Rainbow.
h. Modern Library.
p. Viking: Compass.
Women in Love.
h. Modern Library.
p. introd. Richard Aldington. Viking: Compass.

22 GUILLAUME APOLLINAIRE *Alcools; Poèmes, 1898-1913*. Paris: Mercure de France, 1913.
f. Paris: Gallimard; Le livre de poche, 771.
h. =*Alcools: Poems, 1898-1913*; ed. Francis Steegmuller, trans. William Meredith. New York: Doubleday.

Selected Writings; trans. Roger Shattuck. [Bilingual.] New York: New Directions.

p. *Selected Poems*; trans. Oliver Bernard. Penguin.

American editions

h., p. =*Alcools: Poems, 1898-1913*; ed. Francis Steegmuller; trans. William Meredith. [Bilingual.] Doubleday; Doubleday: Anchor.

h. =*Alcools*; trans. Anne Hyde Greet; introd. Warren Ramsey. [Bilingual.] Berkeley: University of California Press.

p. *Selected Poems of Guillaume Appollinaire*; trans. Oliver Bernard. Penguin.

23 MARCEL PROUST *Du Côté de Chez Swann*. Paris: Grasset, 1913. Forms part of: *À la Recherche du Temps Perdu*, 15 vol., 1913-27. [Proust died 1923.]

f. Paris: Gallimard (15 vol.). Le livre de poche, 1426-7, 1428-9, etc.: to be completed in 8 vol.

h. =*Remembrance of Things Past*; vol. 1-11 trans. C. K. Scott Moncrieff, vol. 12. Stephen Hudson [i.e. Sydney Schiff]. Chatto & Windus.

p. =*Swann's Way*. Penguin.*

Charles Baudelaire, *Les Fleurs du Mal*.

f. Le livre de poche, 677.

h. =*Flowers of Evil*; trans. Florence Louie Friedman. Elek. [Selection.]

p. *Selected Verse*; trans. Francis Scarfe. [Bilingual.] Penguin.

Leo Tolstoy, *War and Peace*.

h. Trans. Louise and Aylmer Maude. O.U.P. (World's Classics).

p. Trans. Rosemary Edmonds. Penguin.

American editions

Du Côté de Chez Swann.

h. =*Remembrance of Things Past*. (2 vols. boxed.) Random House.

h. =*Un Amour de Swann*. Macmillan.

h., p. *Swann's Way*. Modern Library; Modern Library College Editions.

Charles Baudelaire, *Les Fleurs du Mal*.

h. =*Flowers of Evil*; ed. Willian Angeler. [Bilingual.] Fresno, Calif.: Academy Library.

h., p. =*Flowers of Evil*; trans. Edna St. Vincent Millay & George Dillon. Harper; Washington Square Pr.

h., p. =*Flowers of Evil*; ed. Jackson & Marthiel Mathews. [Bilingual.] New Directions.

h. =*Flowers of Evil*. Mount Vernon, N.Y.: Peter Pauper Pr.

h. *One Hundred Poems from Les Fleurs du Mal*; trans. C. F. MacIntyre. [Bilingual.] Berkeley: University of California Pr.

p. *Les Fleurs du Mal*. Chilton.

p. *Selected Flowers of Evil*; ed. Jackson & Marthiel Mathews. [Bilingual.] New Directions.

p. *Selected Verse*; ed. Francis Scarfe. Penguin.

p. *Les Fleurs du Mal*. Doubleday: Anchor. (f.)

p. =*Flowers of Evil and Other Works*; ed. & trans. Wallace Fowlie. Bantam.

Leo Tolstoy, *War and Peace*.

h. (3 vols.) Dutton: Everyman.

h. Grosset.

h. McGraw-Hill.

h. Modern Library.

h. trans. Louise & Aylmer Maude. O.U.P.

h. Simon & Schuster: Inner Sanctum edn.

p. Bantam. (Abridged.)

p. abridged by Edmund Fuller. Dell.

p. trans. Rosemary Edmonds. (2 vols.) Penguin.

p. abridged Edmund Fuller. Englewood Cliffs, N.J.: Scholastic Book Services.

p. trans. Louise and Aylmer Maude; abridged, ed., & introd. Ernest J. Simmons.

24 WILLIAM BUTLER YEATS *Responsibilities*. Dublin: [i.e. Churchtown, Dundrum] Cuala Press, 1914; enlarged edn. London: Macmillan, 1916.

h. *Collected Poems;* 2nd edn. Macmillan.
p. *Selected Poetry*. Macmillan (Pocket Papermacs).
Michael Robartes and the Dancer, 1920.
The Wild Swans at Coole, 1917.
h, p. see 12.

American editions

h. *Collected Poems*. (definitive 2nd edn.) Macmillan.
h. *Poems*; ed. Peter Allt & Russell K. Alspach. (variorum edn.) Macmillan.
p. *Selected Poems*; ed. Macha L. Rosenthal. Macmillan.
p. *The Celtic Twilight and a Selection of Early Poems*; fwd. Wallace Starkie. New American Library: Signet Classics.

25 THOMAS HARDY *Satires of Circumstance*. London: Macmillan, 1914.
h. *Collected Poems*. Macmillan.
p. *Poems*; ed. W. E. Williams. Penguin. [Selection.]

American editions

h. *Complete Works*. St. Martin's Pr.
h. *Collected Poems*. Macmillan.
h. *Love Poems*; ed. Carl J. Weber. St. Martin's Pr.
h. *Selected Poems*; ed. G. M. Young. St. Martin's Pr.
h. *Stories and Poems*; ed. N. V. Meeres. St. Martin's Pr.

26 JAMES JOYCE *Portrait of the Artist as a Young man*. New York: B. W. Huebsch, 1916; London: The Egoist, 1917. [*c.* 1916.] [Serialized in *The Egoist*, 1914-15.]
h. Cape. p. Penguin.
Dubliners, 1914.
h. Cape. p. Penguin.
The Essential James Joyce; ed. Harry Levin, includes both works.
h. Cape. p. Penguin.
Stephen Hero, 1944.
h. rev. edn. Cape, 1956.

American editions

Portrait of the Artist as a Young Man.
h., p. ed. Richard Ellman. Viking; Viking: Compass.

h. *The Portable James Joyce*; ed. Harry Levin. Viking Portable.

p. *Stephen Hero*; introd. Theodore Spencer. (rev. edn.) New Directions.

Dubliners.

h. Modern Library.

h., p. Viking; Viking: Compass.

27 FORD MADOX FORD *The Good Soldier*. London: John Lane (The Bodley Head); New York: John Lane, 1915. [It was announced as "The saddest story" in the publisher's advertisement.]

h. In: *The Bodley Head Ford Madox Ford*, vol. 1. Bodley Head.

p. Penguin.*

Some do not . . . 1924.

h. In: *The Bodley Head Ford Madox Ford*, vol. 3.

No More Parades, 1925.

A Man could Stand Up, 1926.

h. In: *The Bodley Head Ford Madox Ford*, vol. 4.

[These 3 novels form the "Tietjens trilogy" or "Parade's end"; with *Last Post*, 1928, the "Tietjens tetralogy".]

American editions

The Good Soldier.

p. Knopf: Vintage.

Some do not . . .

(See below.)

No More Parades.

h. =*Parade's End.* (rev. edn.) Knopf.

p. =*Parade's End: Parts I and II: Some Do Not and No More Parades*; afterword Arthur Mizener. New American Library: Signet.

p. =*Parade's End: Parts III and IV: A Man Could Stand Up and Last Post*; afterword Arthur Mizener. New American Library: Signet.

28 NORMAN DOUGLAS *South Wind.* London: Secker, 1917.

h. rev. edn. Secker & Warburg, 1946.

p. Penguin.

Richard Aldington, *Pinorman.*

h. Heinemann.*

American editions

South Wind.

h. Modern Library.

p. Bantam.

p. Penguin.

29. PERCY WYNDHAM LEWIS *Tarr*. New York: Knopf; London: *The Egoist*, 1918. 2nd edn: London: Chatto & Windus, 1928.

h. 2nd edn Methuen.*

The Wild Body, 1927.

h. Methuen.*

American edition: none

30 T. S. ELIOT (a) *Prufrock and Other Observations*. London: *The Egoist*, 1917.

h. *Collected Poems*, 1909-62. Faber.

p. *Selected Poems*. Faber.

(b) *The Wasteland*. New York: Boni and Liveright, 1922. London [i.e. Richmond, Surrey]: *Hogarth Press*.

h. as h. above; *The Wasteland and Other Poems*. Faber.

p. *Selected Poems* as above.

American editions

h. *Collected Poems, 1909-1935*. Harcourt.

h. *Collected Poems, 1909-1962*. Harcourt.

h. *Complete Poems and Plays, 1909-1950*. Harcourt.

p. *The Wasteland and Other Poems*. Harcourt: Harvest.

31 PAUL VALÉRY (a) *La Jeune Parque*. Paris: Gallimard, 1917.

f. *Poésies*. Paris: Gallimard.

p. *Selected Writings*. New York: New Directions. [Bilingual, poetry and prose, by various translators.]

(b) *Charmes*. Paris: Gallimard, 1922.

f. *Poésies* as above.

h. *Le Cimetière Marin* (*The Graveyard by the Sea*); trans. C. Day Lewis. [Bilingual.] Secker & Warburg.*

p. *Selected Writings* as above. *French Verse: 4 The Twentieth Century*; ed. Anthony Hartley. [Bilingual.] Penguin, also cont. *Le Cimetière Marin.*

Variété, I-V, 1924-1944.

f. Paris: Gallimard.

h =*Variety*; trans. Malcolm Cowley. New York, Harcourt, Brace*;—*2nd series*; trans. W. A. Bradley. New York: Harcourt, Brace.*

The Collected Works, in Bilingual Edition; ed. Jackson Mathews, Routledge, began to appear in 1958. The vols. published so far do not include the poems.

Correspondance, 1952-57. [See below.]

f. *Lettres à Quelques-uns*. Gallimard.
Correspondance André Gide—Paul Valéry; ed. Robert Mallet. Gallimard.
Correspondance Paul Valéry—Gustave Fourment; ed. Octave Nadal. Gallimard.

Charles Davy's *Words in the Mind* (Chatto & Windus) cont. versions of *La Jeune Parque* and *Le Cimetière Marin.*

American editions

h. *Collected Works*; ed. Jackson Mathews (vols. 3, 4, 7, 10, 12, 13). (Does not include poems.) Pantheon.

p. *Selected Writings*. [Bilingual.] New Directions.

32 GUILLAUME APOLLINAIRE *Calligrammes*. Paris: Mercure de France, 1918.

See 22.

American edition

h. *Selected Writings*; trans. Roger Shattuck. New Directions.

33 GERARD MANLEY HOPKINS *Poems*; ed. Robert Bridges. London: O.U.P., 1918.

h. *Poems*; 1st edn enl. and ed. W. H. Gardner; 3rd edn. O.U.P., 1948.

p. *Poems and Prose*; ed. W. H. Gardner. Penguin.* [Selection.]

The Notebooks and Papers; ed. Humphry House, 1937.

h. *The Journals and Papers*; ed. Christopher Devlin, O.U.P., 1959.

p. *Poems and Prose* as above.

The Letters of Gerard Manley Hopkins to Robert Bridges; ed. Claude Colleer Abbott, 1935.

The Correspondence of Gerard Manley Hopkins and R. W. Dixon; ed. C. C. Abbott, 1935.
h. *The Letters . . . and Correspondence*; ed. C. C. Abbott. 2 vol. O.U.P., 1955.
p. *Poems and Prose* as above.
Further Letters of Gerard Manley Hopkins; ed. C. C. Abbott, 1938.
h. 2nd edn. O.U.P., 1956.
p. *Poems and Prose* as above.

American editions
Poems.
h. *Gerard Manley Hopkins Reader*; ed. John Pick. O.U.P.
h. *Poems*; ed. Robert Bridges & W. H. Gardner. (3rd edn.) O.U.P.
p. *Selected Poems and Prose*; ed. W. H. Gardner. Penguin.
Journals and Papers.
h. ed. Humphry House. O.U.P.
The Letters of Gerard Manley Hopkins to Robert Bridges; ed. C. C. Abbot (bound with *The Correspondence of Gerard Manley Hopkins and Richard Watson*). (2 vols.; rev. ed.) O.U.P.

34 ARTHUR WALEY *A Hundred and Seventy Chinese Poems*. London: Constable, 1918.
h. *Chinese Poems*. Allen and Unwin. [Selection.]
p. *Chinese Poems*. Allen and Unwin (Unwin books).
The Tale of Genji [of Lady Murasaki]. 6 vol., 1925-33.
h. Omnibus edn. Allen and Unwin.
Ezra Pound, *Cathay*, 1915.
Included in: *Personae*, 1952. See (35).

American editions
A Hundred and Seventy Chinese Poems.
h. *Translations from the Chinese*. Knopf.
The Tale of Genji (of Lady Murasaki).
h. Houghton. (2 vols.)
h. Modern Library.
p. Part I & Part II, *The Sacred Tree*. Doubleday: Anchor.
Ezra Pound, *Cathay*.
Included in: *Personae*. See 35.

35 EZRA POUND *Lustra*. London: Elkin Mathews, 1916.
Hugh Selwyn Mauberley. London: Ovid Press, 1920.
h. In: *Personae: Collected Shorter Poems*. Faber, 1952.
h, p. *Selected Poems*; ed. T. S. Eliot. Faber.
Homage to Sextus Propertius, 1919. [In: *Quia pauper Amavi*.]
h. In: *Personae*, 1952, as h. above.

American editions
Lustra.
Hugh Selwyn Mauberley.
h. In: *Personae: Collected Shorter Poems*. New Directions.
p. *Selected Poems*. (rev. ed.) New Directions.
Homage to Sextus Propertius.
h. In: *Personae*, as h. above.

36 WILFRED OWEN *Poems*; ed. Siegfried Sassoon. London: Chatto & Windus, 1920.
h. *Collected Poems*; ed. C. Day Lewis. Chatto & Windus, 1963.

American edition
h., p. *Collected Poems*. New Directions.

37 GILES LYTTON STRACHEY *Eminent Victorians*. London: Chatto & Windus, 1918.
h. Chatto. p. Penguin.*

American editions
h. Modern Library.
h. Gloucester, Mass.: Peter Smith.
p. Putnam: Capricorn.

38 D. H. LAWRENCE *Sea and Sardinia*. New York: Seltzer, 1921. London: Secker, 1923.
h. Heinemann.
p. New York: Viking (Compass); Penguin.*
Birds, Beasts and Flowers, 1923.
In: *Complete Poems*, 1964, vol. 1. See 21.
Norman Douglas, *Alone*, 1921.
h. Chapman & Hall.*

American editions
Sea and Sardinia.
p. Viking: Compass.

Birds, Beasts and Flowers.
h. In: *Complete Poems*; ed. Vivian de Sola Pinto & F. Warren Roberts. Viking. See 21.
p. *Selected Poems.* Viking: Compass.

39 ALDOUS HUXLEY *Crome Yellow.* London: Chatto & Windus, 1921.
h. Chatto & Windus. p. Penguin.
Antic hay, 1923.
h. Chatto & Windus. p. Penguin.
Limbo, 1920.
h. Chatto & Windus.
Mortal coils, 1922.
h. Chatto & Windus. p. Penguin.

American editions
Crome Yellow.
h. Harper.
p. Bantam.
Antic Hay.
h. Modern Library.
h., p. *Antic Hay and The Gioconda Smile*; introd. Martin Green. Harper: Harper's Modern Classics; Harper: Torchbooks.

40 KATHERINE MANSFIELD *The Garden Party, and Other Stories.* London: Constable, 1922.
h. *Collected Stories.* Constable.
p. Penguin.
Christopher Isherwood, *The World in the Evening*, 1954.
h. Methuen.
p. New English Library (Four Square).
Aldous Huxley, *Crome Yellow.* See 39.
Those Barren Leaves, 1925.
h. Chatto & Windus. p. Penguin.

American editions
The Garden Party, and other Stories.
h. *Short Stories.* Knopf.
p. *Stories*; ed. Elizabeth Bowen. Knopf: Vintage.
Aldous Huxley, *Crome Yellow.* See 39.

Those Barren Leaves.
p. Avon.

41 WILLIAM BUTLER YEATS *Later Poems.* London: Macmillan, 1922.
h. *Collected Poems;* 2nd edn. Macmillan.
p. *Selected Poetry.* Macmillan (Pocket Papermacs).
The Trembling of the Veil, 1922.
h. In: *Autobiographies.* Macmillan.
Ezra Pound, *Certain Noble Plays of Japan*; introd. W. B. Yeats, 1916.
h. In: *The Translations of Ezra Pound*; introd. Hugh Kenner. Faber.
p. =*The Classic Noh Theatre of Japan.* New York: New Directions.

American editions

Later Poems.
See 24.
The Trembling of the Veil.
h. *Autobiography.* Macmillan.

42 JAMES JOYCE *Ulysses.* Paris: Shakespeare and Company, 1922.
h. new edn. Bodley Head, 1960.
p. [a few sections only] in: *The Essential James Joyce*; ed. Harry Levin. Penguin.

American edition

h. Random House; Modern Library.

43 RAYMOND RADIGUET *Le Diable au Corps.* Paris: Grasset, 1923.
f. Le livre de poche, 119.
h. =*The Devil in the Flesh*; trans. Kay Boyle. Grey Walls Press.*
p. as above. New York: New American Library (Signet Books).
Le Bal du Comte d'Orgel, 1924.
f. Le livre de poche, 435.
h. =*Count d'Orgel opens the Ball*; trans. Violet Schiff. Harvill Press.*

p. =*Count d'Orgel*; trans. Violet Schiff. New York: Grove Press (Evergreen).

Henri Alain-Fournier, *Le Grand Meaulnes*, 1913.

f. Le livre de poche, 1000.

h. =*The Lost Domain*; trans. Frank Davison. O.U.P. (World's Classics).

Charles Louis Phillippe, *Bubu de Montparnasse*, 1901.

f. Fasquelle.

h. =*Bubu of Montparnasse*; trans. Laurence Vail. Weidenfeld & Nicolson.*

American editions

Le Diable au Corps.

p. =*Devil in the Flesh*. New American Library: Signet.

Le Bal du Comte d'Orgel.

p. =*Count d'Orgel*. Grove: Evergreen.

Henri Alain-Fournier, *Le Grand Meaulnes*.

h. =*The Last Domain*; trans. Frank Davison. O.U.P.: World's Classics.

44 RONALD FIRBANK *The Flower beneath the Foot*. London: Grant Richards, 1923.

h. *The Complete Ronald Firbank*; with a preface by Anthony Powell. Duckworth.

Prancing Nigger, 1924. [In London edn as: *Sorrow in sunlight*.]

Concerning the Eccentricities of Cardinal Pirelli, 1926.

h. *The Complete Ronald Firbank* as h above.

p. *Valmouth*, *Prancing Nigger*, *Concerning the Eccentricities of Cardinal Pirelli*. Penguin.

American editions

The Flower Beneath the Foot.

h. *Complete Ronald Firbank*. New Directions.

Prancing Nigger.

Concerning the Eccentricities of Cardinal Pirelli.

h. *Five novels: Valmouth; Artificial Princess; The Flower Beneath the Foot; Prancing Nigger; Eccentricities of Cardinal Pirelli*. New Directions.

p. *Two Novels: The Flower Beneath the Foot and Prancing Nigger*. New Directions.

45 E. M. FORSTER *A Passage to India*. London: Edward Arnold, 1924.

h. Notes by the author. Dent (Everyman); Arnold.
p. Penguin.

American edition

h. Harcourt: Harbrace Modern Classics.

46 WALLACE STEVENS *Harmonium*. New York: Knopf, 1923; with additional poems, 1926; 1931.

Transport to Summer, 1947.

h. *Collected Poems*. Faber.
p. *Selected Poems*. Faber.

American editions

h. *Collected Poems*. Knopf.
h. *Opus Posthumous*. Knopf.
p. *Poems*; ed. Samuel French Morse. Knopf: Vintage.

47 E. E. CUMMINGS *Tulips and Chimneys*. New York: Seltzer, 1923; Mount Vernon, N.Y.: Golden Eagle Press, 1937.

Is 5. New York: Boni & Liveright, 1926.
(&, 1925; *41 Poems*, 1925).
1 × 1, 1944.

h. *Collected Poems*. New York: Harcourt, Brace; *Selected Poems, 1923-58*. Faber.
p. *Selected Poems, 1923-58*. Penguin.

The Enormous Room, 1922.

h. New York: Modern Library.

Robert Frost, *New Hampshire*.

h. *Complete Poems*. Cape.
p. *Selected Poems*. Penguin.

American editions

h. *Collected Poems*. Harcourt.
h. *E. E. Cummings: A Miscellany Revised*. October House.
h. *Ninety-Five Poems*. Harcourt.
h. *Poems: 1923-1954*. Harcourt.
h. *73 Poems*. (1963) Harcourt.
p. *50 Poems*. Universal Library.
p. *100 Selected Poems*. Grove: Evergreen.

Is 5.
h. Liveright.
One Times One.
h. Harcourt.
The Enormous Room.
h. Liveright.
h. Modern Library.

48 F. SCOTT FITZGERALD *The Great Gatsby.* New York: Scribner, 1925.
h. In: *Bodley Head Scott Fitzgerald*, vol. 1. Bodley Head.
p. Penguin.
This Side of Paradise, 1920.
h. *Bodley Head Scott Fitzgerald*, as above, vol. 3.
p. Penguin.
Mark Twain, *Huckleberry Finn.*
h, p. *Tom Sawyer and Huckleberry Finn.* Dent (Everyman, Everyman Paperbacks).
Walt Whitman, *Leaves of Grass.*
h. Dent (Everyman).
p. Cornell University Press with O.U.P.

American editions
The Great Gatsby.
h., p. Scribner; Scribner Library.
h. *Three Novels: The Great Gatsby; Tender is the Night; The Last Tycoon.* Scribner.
This Side of Paradise.
p. Scribner Library.
Mark Twain, *Huckleberry Finn.*
(The following = *The Adventures of Huckleberry Finn*):
h. Dial: Heritage.
h. Dodd: Great Illustrated Classics.
h. Dufour.
h. Grosset.
h. Harper: Harper's Modern Classics.
h. Macmillan.
(The following = *Huckleberry Finn*):
h. Dutton.
h. In: *Four Great American Novels*; ed. Raymond W. Short.

h. ed. Robert J. Dixson. (adapted) Regents Publishing Co.
h. (adapted) Scott, Foresman.
(The following = *The Adventures of Huckleberry Finn*):
p. Airmont Publishing Co.
p. introd. Newton Arvin. Collier.
p. introd. Hamilton Hill. (Facsimile of first printing.) San Francisco: Chandler Publishing Co.
p. ed. Wallace Stegner. Dell.
p. Dolphin Books.
p. ed. Lionel Trilling. Harcourt.
p. Penguin.
p. ed. Henry Nash Smith. Houghton: Riverside; Houghton: Riverside Literature edn.
p. Englewood Cliffs, N. J.: Scholastic Book Services.
p. afterword G. P. Elliott. New American Library: Signet Classics.
p. Washington Square Pr.; ed. Harry Shefter with Hortense H. Lewisohn & Duke H. Shirmer. Washington Square Pr.
(The following = *Huckleberry Finn*):
p. ed. Ralph Cohen. Bantam.
p. ed. Leo Marx. Bobbs-Merrill.
p. *Huckleberry Finn: Text, Sources, and Criticism*; ed. Sculley Bradley, Richmond C. Beatty, & E. Hudson Long. Norton.
p. *The Portable Mark Twain* (selections from *Huckleberry Finn, The Mysterious Stranger and others*). Viking Portable.
p. Harcourt.

Walt Whitman, *Leaves of Grass*.
h. *Collected Writings*; ed. Gay W. Allen & Sculley Bradley. New York University Pr.
h. *Complete Poetry, Selected Prose and Letters*; ed. Emory Holloway. Random House.
h. Doubleday.
h. Dutton: Everyman. (rev. edn.)
h. Modern Library.
h. ed. Harold W. Blodgett & Sculley Bradley. New York University Pr.
h., p. ed. Malcolm Cowley. Viking; Viking: Compass.

h., p. *Leaves of Grass and Selected Prose*; ed. John Kouwenhoven. Modern Library.
h. comp. Lawrence C. Powell. Crowell.
h. *Poems: Selections with Critical Aids*; ed. Gay W. Allen & Charles T. Davis. New York University Pr.
h., p. *The Portable Walt Whitman* (selections from *Leaves of Grass* and others); ed. Mark Van Doren. Viking Portable.
p. Dolphin.
p. (1860 edn.) Ithaca, N.Y.: Cornell University Pr.
p. introd. Gay W. Allen. New American Library: Signet Classics.
p. *Leaves of Grass and Selected Prose*; ed. Sculley Bradley. Holt.
p. *Complete Poetry and Selected Prose*; ed. James E. Miller, Jr. Houghton: Riverside.

49, 50 ERNEST HEMINGWAY *In Our Time*. Paris: William Bird (Three Mountains Press), 1924; New York: Boni & Liveright, 1925; New York: Scribner, 1930 [with additions].
h. In: *The Essential Hemingway*. Cape.
p. as above. Penguin.
Men Without Women, 1927.
h. Cape. p. Penguin.
(Also 4 stories included in *The Essential Hemingway*.)
The Sun also Rises, 1926.
h. =*Fiesta*. Cape. p. Pan Books.
(Also included in *The Essential Hemingway*.)
Mark Twain, *Huckleberry Finn*. See 48.
Gertrude Stein, *Three Lives*.
h. New York: New Directions.
p. New York: Vintage.
Sherwood Anderson, *Winesburg, Ohio*.
h. New York: Modern Library.
p. Penguin*; New York: Viking (Compass).

American editions

In Our Time.
h., p. Scribner.

p. *Big Two-Hearted River*. In: *The Hemingway Reader*; ed. Charles Poore. Scribner.

Men without Women.

h. Scribner.

The Sun Also Rises.

h., p. Scribner.

p. In: *The Hemingway Reader*; ed. Charles Poore. Scribner.

Mark Twain, *Huckleberry Finn*. See 48.

Gertrude Stein, *Three Lives.*

h. New Directions.

p. Knopf: Vintage.

Sherwood Anderson, *Winesburg, Ohio.*

h., p. *The Portable Sherwood Anderson*; ed. Horace Gregory. Viking Portable.

h. Modern Library.

h., p. *Short Stories*; ed. Maxwell Geismar. Hill & Wang,

p. Viking: Compass.

51 ANDRÉ GIDE *Si le Grain ne Meurt*. Paris: Gallimard, 1926. [Given as 1924 in the book itself.]

f. Gallimard.

h. *If it Die*; trans. Dorothy Bussy. Secker & Warburg.

p. as above. Penguin.*

Corydon, 1911. [Published anonymously as: *C.R.D.N.*]

f. Gallimard.

h. trans. "P.B.". Secker & Warburg.

Journal, *1889-1939*, *1939-49*, 1939-50.

f. Gallimard. (Éd. Pléiade.)

h. = *The Journals*; trans. Justin O'Brien. 4 vols. Secker & Warburg.

American editions

Si le Grain ne Meurt.

p. = *If it Die*. Knopf: Vintage.

Corydon.

h., p. = *Corydon*. Farrar, Straus; Farrar, Straus: Noonday.

Journal, *1889-1939*, *1939-49*, *1939-50*.

h. = *Journals*. (4 vols.) vol. 1, 1889-1913; vol. 2, 1914-

1927; vol. 3, 1928-1939; vol. 4, 1939-1949, 1947-1951. Knopf.

p. =*Journals: 1889-1949*. (2 vols.) ed. Justin O'Brien. vol. 1, 1889-1924; vol. 2, 1924-1949. Knopf: Vintage.

52 WILLIAM PLOMER *Turbott Wolfe*. London: L. & V. Woolf (Hogarth Press), 1926 [dated 1925].

h. repr. with new foreword by Laurens Van der Post. Hogarth Press, 1965.

American edition

h. William Morrow.

53 WILLIAM SOMERSET MAUGHAM *The Casuarina Tree*. London: Heinemann, 1926.

h. Heinemann.

Also in: *Complete Short Stories*. 3 vol. Heinemann.

p. In: *Collected Short Stories*. 4 vol. Penguin.

Ah King, 1933.

In the collections named above.

Ashenden, 1928.

h. Heinemann.

Also in the collections named above.

Cakes and Ale, 1930.

h. Heinemann. p. Penguin.

American editions

The Casuarina Tree.

Ah King.

Ashenden.

h. *Best Short Stories*. Modern Library.

h. *Complete Short Stories*. (2 vols.) vol 1, *East and West*; vol. 2, *The World Over*. Doubleday.

p. *Ashenden*. (re-issue.) Avon.

p. *Favorite Stories*. Avon.

p. *Stories of the East*. Ballantine.

Cakes and Ale.

h. Modern Library.

p. Pocket Books. (re-issue.)

54 VIRGINIA WOOLF *To the Lighthouse*. London: Hogarth Press, 1927.

h. Hogarth Press; Dent (Everyman).
p. Penguin; Dent (Everyman Paperbacks).

American edition

h., p. Harcourt: Harbrace Modern Classics; Harcourt: Harvest.

55 ANDRÉ BRETON *Nadja*. Paris: Gallimard, 1928.
f. Gallimard; Le livre de poche, 1233.
h. trans. Richard Howard. Gloucester, Mass.: Peter Smith.
p. as above. New York: Grove Press (Evergreen).
Les pas Perdus, 1924.
f. Gallimard.
Louis Aragon, *Paysan de Paris*.
f. Gallimard.

American editions

Nadja.
h. trans. Richard Howard. Gloucester, Mass.: Peter Smith.
p. Grove: Evergreen.

56 WILLIAM BUTLER YEATS (a) *The Tower*. London: Macmillan, 1928. [Appeared in: *October Blast*. Dublin: Cuala Press, 1927.] (b) *The Winding Stair*. New York: Fountain Press, 1929. [Dated 1928; distributed in U.S.A. by Random House, in G.B. by Grant Richards and Humphrey Toulmin. 1st London edn, Macmillan, 1933.]
Words for Music Perhaps. Dublin, Cuala Press, 1932.
h. *Collected Poems;* 2nd edn. Macmillan.
p. *Selected Poetry*. Macmillan (Pocket Paperbacks).
Autobiographies, 1926; 1938; 1955.
h. Macmillan.
p. *Selected Prose*; ed. A. Norman Jeffares. Macmillan (Pocket Papermacs).
A Packet for Ezra Pound, 1929. [Partly reprinted in *Words for Music Perhaps* and *A Vision* (1937)].

American editions

See 24, 41.

57 D. H. LAWRENCE *Lady Chatterley's Lover*. Florence: privately printed, 1928.
h. Heinemann, 1960. [Unexpurgated edn.]
p. Penguin, 1960. [Unexpurgated edn.]
The Fox, 1923.
St. Mawr, 1925.
The Man Who Died, 1929.
h. *The Short Novels*. 2 vol. Heinemann.
p. *St. Mawr, and The Virgin and the Gypsy*. Penguin.*
The Woman Who Rode Away, and Other Stories. Penguin.*
Letters; ed. Aldous Huxley, 1932.
h. *Collected Letters*; ed. Harry T. Moore. 2 vols. Heinemann, 1962. [Not complete: See *Times Literary Supplement*, 27.iv.1962, for a discussion of this.]
p. *Selected Letters*; ed. Richard Aldington. Penguin, 1950.
Virginia Woolf, *The Common Reader*: series 1 and 2, 1925, 1932.
h. Hogarth Press. p. Pelican.*

American editions

Lady Chatterley's Lover.
h. Modern Library.
p. Grove: Evergreen (Black Cat Series).
p. Pocket Books. (re-issue.)
p. New American Library: Signet (authorized expurgated edn.)
p. New American Library: Signet (authorized unexpurgated edn.)
The Fox
p. In: *Four Short Novels* (*Love Among the Haystacks, The Ladybird, The Fox, The Captain's Doll*). Viking: Compass.
St. Mawr.
The Man Who Died.
p. *St. Mawr and The Man Who Died*. Knopf: Vintage.
Letters.
h. *Selected Letters*; ed. Diana Trilling. Farrar, Straus.
Virginia Woolf, *The Common Reader*: series 1 and 2.
p. =*First Common Reader*. Harcourt: Harvest.
p. =*Second Common Reader*. Harcourt: Harvest.

58 EVELYN WAUGH *Decline and Fall.* London: Chapman & Hall, 1928.

h. rev. edn Chapman & Hall, 1962.
p. Penguin.

Vile Bodies, 1930.

h. reset edn with introd. by author, Chapman & Hall, 1965.
p. Penguin.

Black Mischief, 1932.

h. New edn. Chapman & Hall, 1962.
p. Penguin.

Scoop, 1938.

h. New edn. Chapman & Hall, 1962.
p. Penguin.

The Loved One, 1948.

h. new edn. Chapman & Hall, 1965.
p. Penguin.

A Handful of Dust, 1934.

h. New edn [with alternative ending]. Chapman & Hall, 1964
p. Penguin.

American editions

Decline and Fall.

p. *A Handful of Dust and Decline and Fall.* Dell.
p. Universal Library.

Vile Bodies.

h. Little, Brown.
p. *Vile Bodies and Black Mischief.* Dell.

Black Mischief.

h. Little, Brown.
p. *Vile Bodies and Black Mischief.* Dell.

Scoop.

p. *Scoop and Put out More Flags.* Dell.

The Loved One.

h. Little, Brown.
p. Dell.
p. Knopf: Vintage.

A Handful of Dust.

p. *A Handful of Dust and Decline and Fall.* Dell.

59 HENRY GREEN *Living*. London & Toronto: Dent, 1929.
h. Hogarth Press.
Loving, 1945.
h. Hogarth Press.
p. Penguin.* [Re-issue likely.]
American edition: none

60 ERNEST HEMINGWAY *A Farewell to Arms*. New York: Scribner; London: Cape, 1929.
h. Cape. p. Penguin.
To Have and Have Not, 1937.
h. Cape. p. Penguin.
Across the River and into the Trees, 1950.
h. Cape.
American editions
A Farewell to Arms.
h., p. Scribner; Scribner: Scribner Library.
p. sel. In: *The Hemingway Reader*; ed. Charles Poore. Scribner: Scribner Library.
To Have and Have Not.
h. Scribner.
Across the River and Into the Trees.
h. Scribner.

61 ROBERT GRAVES *Goodbye to All That*. London: Cape; New York: J. Cape & H. Smith, 1929.
h. rev. edn Cassell, 1957.
p. Penguin.
Poems, 1929, 1929.
h. *Collected Poems, 1959*. Cassell.
p. *Selected Poems*. Penguin.
N.B. In later collections, Graves has suppressed many of his earlier poems.
American editions
Goodbye to All That.
p. Doubleday: Anchor.
Poems, 1929
p. *The Poems of Robert Graves: Chosen by Himself*. Doubleday: Anchor.

62 JEAN COCTEAU *Les Enfants Terribles*. Paris: Grasset, 1929.

f. Le livre de poche, 399.

h. =*Children of the Game*; trans. Rosamund Lehmann. Harvill Press.*

p. as above. Penguin.

Le Potomak, 1919.

f. Paris: Stock.

Le Grand Écart, 1923.

f. Paris: Stock.

h. =*The Grand Écart*; trans. Lewis Galantière. New York: Putnam, 1925.*

Thomas l'Imposteur, 1923.

f. Le livre de poche, 244.

h. =*Thomas the Impostor*; trans. Lewis Galantière. New York, London: Appleton, 1925.*

=*The Impostor*; trans. Dorothy Williams. Owen, 1955.

p. as above. Brown, Watson.

Le Rappel à l'Ordre, 1926.

f. Stock.

h. =*A Call to Order*; trans. Rollo H. Myers. Faber & Gwyer, 1926.*

Opium, 1930.

f. Stock.

h. trans. E. Boyd. Longmans, 1932*; Allen & Unwin*; trans. Margaret Crosland & Sinclair Road. Owen, 1957.

Georges Bataille [as Lord Auch], *Histoire de l'Oeil*, 1929.*

American editions

Les Enfants Terribles.

h. =*The Holy Terrors*. New Directions.

p. In: *Jean Cocteau: Five Plays* (*The Eagle with Two Heads; Antigone; Orphée*, trans. Carl Wildman; *Intimate Relations*, trans. Charles Frank; *The Holy Terrors*, trans. Edwin O. Marsh). Hill & Wang: Dramabooks.

Thomas l'Imposteur.

h. =*The Imposter;* trans. Dorothy Williams. Farrar, Strauss.

p. (f.) Macmillan.

Opium.
p. trans. Margaret Crosland and Sinclair Read. Grove.

63 IVY COMPTON-BURNETT *Brothers and Sisters.* London: Heath Cranton, 1929; New York: Harcourt, Brace, 1929.
h. Gollancz.
Dolores, 1911.
h. Blackwood.*
Pastors and Masters, 1925.
h. Gollancz.
American edition: none

64 HART CRANE *The Bridge.* Paris: Black Sun Press; New York: Liveright, 1930.
h. *Collected Poems*; ed. Waldo Frank. New York: Liveright.
p. *Complete Poems*; ed. Waldo Frank. New York: Doubleday (Anchor).
White Buildings, 1926.
See above.
Arthur Rimbaud, *Le Bateau Ivre.*
f, p. =*A Season in Hell and The Drunken Boat*; trans. Louise Varèse. [Bilingual.] New York: New Directions.
See also 6.
American editions
h. *Collected Poems: Including The Bridge*; ed. Waldo Frank. Liveright, or Tudor.
p. *Complete Poems*; ed. Waldo Frank. Doubleday: Anchor.
Arthur Rimbaud, *Le Bateau Ivre.*
p. =*A Season in Hell and the Drunken Boat.* [Bilingual.] trans. Louise Varèse. New Directions.
See also 6.

65 T. S. ELIOT *Ash Wednesday.* New York: Fountain Press; London: Faber, 1930.
The Hollow Men, 1925. [In: *Poems, 1909-25.*]
See 30.
After Strange Gods, 1934.
H. Faber.*

Dante Alighieri, *L'Inferno*.

h. = *The Inferno*. [Bilingual.] Dent (Temple Classics). [The edn Eliot used.]

American editions

Ash Wednesday.

The Hollow Men.

See 30.

Dante Alighieri, *L'Inferno*.

h. *The Divine Comedy*; trans. Dorothy L. Sayers. (3 vols.) Basic Books.

h. *The Divine Comedy*; trans. J. B. Fletcher. Columbia University Pr.

h. *The Divine Comedy*. Dutton. (3 vols.) [Bilingual.] Dutton: Everyman.

h., p. *The Divine Comedy*. Modern Library.

h. *The Divine Comedy*; trans. M. B. Anderson. O.U.P.: World's Classics.

h. *The Divine Comedy*; ed. Lawrence G. White. Tudor.

h. *Inferno*; ed. Kenelm Foster; trans. Warwick Chipman. O.U.P.

h. *Inferno*; trans. L. Lockert. Princeton University Pr.

h. *Inferno*; trans. John Ciardi. Rutgers University Pr.

p. *The Divine Comedy*; trans. & ed. Thomas G. Bergin. Appleton.

p. *The Divine Comedy*; trans. John D. Sinclair. Vol 1, *Inferno*. [Bilingual.] Galaxy Books.

p. *The Divine Comedy*; ed. & trans. H. R. Huse. Holt.

p. *The Divine Comedy*; introd. C. H. Grandgent; trans. Carlyle-Wicksteed. Knopf: Vintage: Modern Library.

p. *The Divine Comedy: I* (*Inferno*); trans. Dorothy L. Sayers. Penguin.

p. *The Inferno*; introd. Bernard Stampler. Collier.

p. *The Inferno*; trans. John Ciardi. Mentor.

p. *The Portable Dante* (*The Divine Comedy; The New Life*, and others); ed. Paolo Milano. Viking: Viking Portable.

66 EZRA POUND *A Draft of XVI Cantos*. Paris: Three Mountains Press, 1925. *A Draft of the Cantos 17-27*. London: John Rodker,

1928. *A Draft of XXX Cantos*. Paris: Hours Press, 1930; London: Faber, 1933.

Pisan Cantos, 1948. See 98.

h. *The Cantos*; new collected edn. Faber, 1964.

American editions

h. *Cantos* (*Cantos* 1 through 84). (rev. edn.) New Directions.

h. *The Cantos* (1-95). (the first six sections of the *Cantos*). New Directions.

67 EDITH SITWELL *Collected Poems*. Boston: Houghton, Mifflin; London: Duckworth, 1930.

h. *Collected Poems*. Macmillan, 1957.

p. *Selected Poems*. Penguin*;

Poems New and Old. Faber (Sesame books);

Selected Poems; ed. John Lehmann. Macmillan (Papermacs), 1965.

Christina Rossetti, *Goblin Market*.

h. *Goblin Market, Prince's Progress and Other Poems*. O.U.P. (World's Classics).

American edition

Collected Poems.

h. Vanguard.

68 ANTOINE DE SAINT-ÉXUPERY *Vol de Nuit*. Paris: Gallimard, 1931.

f. Le livre de poche, 3.

h. =*Night Flight*; trans. Stuart Gilbert. Century Co.*

p. as above. New York: New American Library (Signet Classics).

Terre des Hommes, 1939.

f. Le livre de poche, 68.

h. =*Wind, Sand and Stars*; trans. Lewis Galantière. New York: Harcourt, Brace.

American editions

Vol de Nuit.

p. =*Night Flight*; fwd. André Gide. New American Library: Signet Classics.

p. ed. Edgar M. Bowman. (f.) Harper.

Terre des Hommes.
h. =*Wind, Sand and Stars*. Harcourt: Harbrace Modern Classics.

69 WILLIAM FAULKNER *Sanctuary*. New York: J. Cape & H. Smith; London: Chatto & Windus, 1931.
h. Chatto & Windus. p. Penguin.
The Sound and the Fury, 1929.
h. Chatto & Windus. p. Penguin.
Light in August, 1932.
h. Chatto & Windus. p. Penguin.
Absalom, Absalom, 1936.
h. Chatto & Windus.
These 13, 1931.
h. In: *Collected Short Stories*, vol. 2. Chatto & Windus.
Percy Wyndham Lewis, *Men Without Art*, 1934.
h. New York: Russell.

American editions
Sanctuary.
h. Random House.
h. Modern Library.
p. *Sanctuary and Requiem for a Nun*. New American Library: Signet.
The Sound and the Fury.
h. *The Sound and the Fury and As I Lay Dying*. Modern Library.
p. Knopf: Vintage.
Light in August.
h. Modern Library.
p. Modern Library College Editions.
Absalom, Absalom.
h. Modern Library.
Percy Wyndham Lewis, *Men Without Art.*
h. Russell.

70 VIRGINIA WOOLF *The Waves*. London: L. & V. Woolf (Hogarth Press), 1931.
h. Hogarth Press. p. Penguin.

American editions
h. Harcourt.
p. *Jacob's Room and The Waves*. Harcourt: Harvest.

71 EDMUND WILSON *Axel's Castle*. New York, London: Scribner, 1931.
h, p. Scribner. p. Collins (Fontana).
To the Finland Station, 1940.
h. Secker & Warburg.* p. Collins (Fontana).
Sir Maurice Bowra, *The Heritage of Symbolism.*
h. Macmillan.
The Creative Experiment.
p. Grove Press (Evergreen).

American editions

Axel's Castle.
h., p. Scribner; Scribner: Scribner Library.
To the Finland Station.
h. Gloucester, Mass.: Peter Smith.
p. Doubleday: Anchor.
Sir Maurice Bowra, *The Heritage of Symbolism.*
h. St. Martin's Pr.
p. Schocken Books.

72 T. S. ELIOT *Selected Essays*. London: Faber; New York: Harcourt, Brace, 1932.
h. 3rd edn. Faber, 1951.
p. *Selected Prose*. Penguin.
Elizabethan Dramatists. Faber.
The Sacred Wood, 1920.
h, p. Methuen.

American editions

Selected Essays.
h. (rev. edn., 1950) Harcourt.
Elizabethan Dramatists.
p. =*Essays on Elizabethan Drama.* Harcourt: Harvest.
The Sacred Wood.
p. (7th edn., 1950) Barnes & Noble: University Paperbacks.

73 W. H. AUDEN *The Orators*. London: Faber, 1932.
[Included in: *Poems*, New York: Random House, 1934.]
Poems, 1930; 1933.
h. *Collected Shorter Poems, 1930-44*. Faber, 1950.

Collected Poetry. New York: Random House, 1945.

p. *W. H. Auden*: a selection by the author. Penguin.

N.B. Earlier poems by Auden in later collections have often been revised or omitted by Auden himself, so the first editions are not superseded by the later.

American edition

h. In: *Collected Poetry*. Random House.

74 LOUIS-FERDINAND CÉLINE *Voyage au Bout de la Nuit*. Paris: Denoël et Steele, 1932.

f. Le livre de poche, 147-148.

h.p. = *Journey to the End of the Night*; trans. John H. P. Marks. Chatto & Windus*; New York: New Directions.

Mort à Credit, 1936.

f. Le livre de poche, 295-296.

h. = *Death on the Instalment Plan*; trans. John H. P. Marks. Chatto & Windus*; New York: New Directions.

Henry Miller, *Tropic of Cancer*.

h. Calder. p. Panther.

George Orwell, *Down and Out in Paris and London*.

See 93.

American editions

Voyage au Bout de la Nuit.

p. = *Journey to the End of Night*; trans. J. H. Marks. New Directions.

Mort à Credit.

h. = *Death on the Installment Plan*. New Directions.

Henry Miller, *Tropic of Cancer*.

h., p. Grove; Grove: Black Cat Series.

George Orwell, *Down and Out in Paris and London*.

See 93.

75 ALDOUS HUXLEY *Brave New World*. London: Chatto & Windus; New York: Doubleday, Doran, 1932.

h. Chatto & Windus. p. Penguin.

Antic Hay, 1923. See 39.

Point Counter Point, 1928.

h. Chatto & Windus. p. Penguin.

Texts and Pretexts, 1932.
h. Chatto & Windus.
Eyeless in Gaza, 1936.
h. Chatto & Windus. p. Penguin.
Time Must Have a Stop, 1945.
h. Chatto & Windus.

American editions

Brave New World.
h. (1932 edn.) Harper.
p. *Brave New World and Brave New World Revisited.* Harper: Torchbooks.
p. Bantam.
Antic Hay. See 39.
Point Counter Point.
h., p. Harper; Harper: Torchbooks.
h. Harper: Harper's Modern Classics.
h. Modern Library.
p. Avon.
p. Harper: Perennial Library.
Texts and Pretexts.
p. Norton.
Eyeless in Gaza.
h. Harper.
p. Bantam.
Time Must Have a Stop.
h. Harper.
p. (re-issue.) Berkly Publishing Co.

76 NATHANAEL WEST *Miss Lonelyhearts*. New York: Liveright, 1933.
h. *Complete Works*. New York: Farrar, Straus; Secker & Warburg.*
p. *Miss Lonelyhearts and A Cool Million*. Penguin.
The Day of the Locust, 1939.
h. *Complete Works* as above.
p. *The Day of the Locust and The Dream Life of Balso Snell.* Penguin.
F. Scott Fitzgerald, *The Great Gatsby*. See 48.

American editions

Miss Lonelyhearts.

h. *Complete Works.* Farrar, Straus.

p. (re-issue.) Avon.

p. *Miss Lonelyhearts and The Day of the Locust.* New Directions.

The Day of the Locust.

p. Bantam.

See above.

F. Scott Fitzgerald, *The Great Gatsby.* See 48.

77 ANDRÉ MALRAUX *La Condition Humaine.* Paris: Gallimard, 1933.

f. Le livre de poche, 27.

h. =*Man's Estate*; trans. Alistair Macdonald. Methuen.*

p. as above. Penguin.

La Voie Royale, 1930. [=*Les Puissances du Désert,* vol. 1.]

f. Le livre de poche, 161-163.

h. =*The Royal Way*; trans. Stuart Gilbert. Methuen, 1935.*

p. as above. New York: Random House (Vintage Books).

American editions

La Condition Humaine.

h., p. =*Man's Fate.* Modern Library; Modern Library College Editions.

La Voie Royale.

p. (f.) Macmillan.

p. *The Royal Way*; trans. Stuart Gilbert. Knapf: Vintage.

78 DYLAN THOMAS *Eighteen Poems.* London: *Sunday Referee,* Parton Bookshop, 1934.

Twenty-five Poems, 1936.

The Map of Love, 1939.

h. *Collected Poems, 1934-52.* Dent.

p. *Dylan Thomas Miscellany: Poems, Stories, Broadcasts.* Dent (Aldine paperbacks). [A small selection.]

American edition

h. *Collected Poems.* New Directions.

79 F. SCOTT FITZGERALD *Tender is the Night*. New York: Scribner, 1934.

h. In: *Bodley Head Scott Fitzgerald*, vol. 2. Bodley Head.

p. with the author's final revision; preface by Malcolm Cowley. Penguin.

American editions

h., p. Scribner; Scribner: Scribner Library.

80 HENRY JAMES *The Art of the Novel*. New York, London: Scribner, 1934.

h, p. Scribner.

American editions

h., p. introd. R. P. Blackmur. Scribner; Scribner: Scribner Library.

h. Gloucester, Mass.: Peter Smith.

81 MARIANNE MOORE *Selected Poems*. New York: Macmillan; London: Faber, 1935.

The Pangolin, 1936.

h. *Collected Poems*. Faber, 1951.

American editions

h. *Collected Poems*. Macmillan.

p. *The Marianne Moore Reader*. Viking: Compass.

82 HENRY DE MONTHERLANT *Les Jeunes Filles*. Paris: Grasset, 1936-39.

f. *Les Jeunes Filles*. Le livre de poche, 43.
Pitié pour les Femmes. As above, 47.
Le Démon du Bien. As above, 48.
Les Lépreuses. As above, 49.

h. =*Pity for Women*. (Pt. I. *Young girls*; trans. Thomas McGreevy. Pt. II. *Pity for Women*; trans. John Rodker.) Routledge & Kegan Paul, 1937.*
=*The Lepers*. (Bk. I. *The Demon of Good*. Bk. II. *The Lepers*; trans. John Rodker.) Routledge & Kegan Paul, 1940.*

A new edition of the four novels constituting *Les Jeunes Filles* is announced by Weidenfeld & Nicolson as part of a uniform edition of Montherlant.

Les Célibataires, 1934.
f. Le livre de poche, 397.
h. =*The Bachelors*; trans. Terence Kilmartin. Weidenfeld & Nicolson.

Simone de Beauvoir, *Le Deuxième Sexe*, 1949.
f. Gallimard.
h. =*The Second Sex*; trans. H. M. Parshley. Cape.
p. vol. 1=*A History of Sex*, now *Nature of the Second Sex*. Vol. 2=*The Second Sex*; trans. H. M. Parshley. New English Library (Four Square).

American editions

Simone de Beauvoir, *Le Deuxième Sexe*.
h. =*The Second Sex*; trans. H. M. Parshley. Knopf.
p. =*The Second Sex*. Bantam.

83 HENRI MICHAUX (a) *Voyage en Grande Garabagne*. Paris: Gallimard, 1936.
(b) *Au pays de la Magie*. Paris: Gallimard, 1941.
f. In: *Ailleurs*. Paris: Gallimard.
h. *Selected Writings*; trans. Richard Ellman. [Bilingual.] New York: New Directions; Routledge and Kegan Paul.* [Selections from 7 works.]

Exorcismes, 1943.
f. In: *Épreuves, Exorcismes*. Paris: Gallimard.

American editions

(a) *Voyage en Grande Garabagne*.
(b) *Au pays de la Magie*.
h. *Selected Writings*; trans. Richard Ellman. New Directions.

84 JEAN-PAUL SARTRE *La Nausée*. Paris: Gallimard, 1938.
f. Le livre de poche, 160.
h. =*Nausea*; trans. Lloyd Alexander. Hamish Hamilton.
p. as above. New York: New Directions; trans. Robert Baldick. Penguin, 1965.

Le mur, 1939.
f. Le livre de poche, 33.
h. =*Intimacy, and Other Stories*; trans. Lloyd Alexander. Spearman.
p. New York: Berkley.

Huis Clos, 1944.
f. Le livre de poche, 1132.
h. In *Two Plays*; trans. Stuart Gilbert. Hamish Hamilton.
p. =*In Camera*, in: *Three European Plays*; trans. E. Martin Browne. Penguin.

American editions

La Nausée.
h., p. =*Nausea*; trans. Lloyd Alexander. New Directions.

Le mur.
h. =*Intimacy*. New Directions.
h. =*Intimacy*. Hackensack, N.J.: Wehman Brothers.
p. =*Intimacy and Other Stories*; trans. Lloyd Alexander. Berkley.

Huis Clos.
h. ed. Jacques Hardré and George B. Daniel. (f.) Appleton.
h. =*No Exit*, in *No Exit and the Flies*; trans. Stuart Gilbert. Knopf.
p. =*No Exit*, in *No Exit and Three Other Plays*; trans. Stuart Gilbert. Knopf: Vintage.

85 LOUIS MACNEICE *Autumn Journal*. London: Faber, 1939.
h. Faber.
p. *Selected Poems*: selected by W. H. Auden. Faber, 1964.

The Earth Compels, 1938.

Plant and Phantom, 1941.
h. *Collected Poems, 1925-1948*. Faber.
p. *Selected Poems* as above.

Springboard: Poems, 1941-1944, 1944.
h. Faber; also *Collected Poems* as above.
p. *Selected poems* as above.

Holes in the Sky: Poems, 1944-47, 1948.
h. Faber; also *Collected Poems* as above.
p. *Selected Poems* as above.

(with W. H. Auden) *Letters from Iceland*, 1937.
h. Faber.*

American editions

h. *Collected Poems, 1925-1948*. O.U.P.
h. *Eighty-five Poems*. O.U.P.

86 CHRISTOPHER ISHERWOOD *Goodbye to Berlin*. London: Hogarth Press, 1939.

h. Hogarth Press. p. Penguin.

The Memorial, 1932.

h. Hogarth Press.

Mr. Norris changes Trains, 1935.

h. Hogarth Press. p. Penguin.

Lions and Shadows, 1935.

h. Hogarth Press.*

p. New English Library (Four Square).

(with W. H. Auden) *Journey to a War*, 1939.

h. Faber.*

American editions

Goodbye to Berlin.

p. *The Berlin Stories* (*Goodbye to Berlin and The Last of Mr. Norris*). New Directions.

The Memorial.

h. New Directions.

Lions and Shadows.

h. New Directions.

87 JAMES JOYCE *Finnegans Wake*. London: Faber; New York: Viking Press, 1939. [Parts of *Finnegans Wake* appeared before 1939 as: *Work in Progress*, 1928-30; *Anna Livia Plurabelle*, 1928; *Tales told of Shem and Shaun*, 1929; *Haveth Childers Everywhere*, 1930; and in various periodicals from 1924.]

h. (re-set.) Faber, 1950.

p. [a few sections only] in: *The Essential James Joyce*. (See 42.)

American editions

h., p. Viking; Viking: Compass.

h. *First-Draft Version of Finnegans Wake*; ed. David Hyman. Austin: University of Texas Pr.

h. *Passages from Finnegans Wake: A Free Adaptation for the Theater*; ed. Mary Manning. Cambridge, Mass.: Harvard University Pr.

h. selections In: *The Portable James Joyce*; ed. Harry Levin. Viking.

88 GRAHAM GREENE *The Power and the Glory*. London: Heinemann, 1940.

h. Heinemann. p. Penguin.

Brighton Rock, 1938.

h. Heinemann. p. Penguin.

American editions

The Power and the Glory.

h., p. Viking; Viking: Compass.

Brighton Rock.

h., p. Viking; Viking: Compass.

89 ARTHUR KOESTLER *Darkness at Noon*; trans. Daphne Hardy. London: Cape, 1940.

h. Cape. p. Penguin.

Spanish Testament, 1937. [English adaptation of *Menschenopfer unerhört*.]

h. Gollancz.*

Dialogue with Death; trans. Trevor & Phyllis Blewitt, 1942. [Part of *Spanish Testament*.]

h. Collins, Hamish Hamilton. p. Penguin.*

American editions

Darkness at Noon.

h. trans. Daphne Hardy. Macmillan.

h. Modern Library.

p. fwd. Peter Viereck. New American Library: Signet Classics.

Dialogue with Death.

p. Macmillan.

90 W. H. AUDEN *Another Time*. London: Faber; New York: Random House, 1940.

See 73.

New Year Letter, 1941.

h. Faber.

The Sea and the Mirror; appeared in: *For the Time Being*, 1944; it was reprinted in *Collected Poetry*. (See 73.)

American edition

Another Time.

See 73.

91 STEPHEN SPENDER *Ruins and Visions*. London: Faber, 1942.
h. *Collected Poems, 1928-53*. Faber.
p. *Selected Poems*. Faber.
The Still Centre, 1939.
See above.

American editions
h. *Collected Poems*. Random House.
h., p. *Selected Poems*. Random House.

92 T. S. ELIOT *Four Quartets*. New York: Harcourt, Brace, 1943; London: Faber, 1944.
[*Burnt Norton*, 1936; *East Coker*, 1940; *Dry Salvages*, 1941; *Little Gidding*, 1942.]
h, p. Faber.

American editions
h. Harcourt.
h. In: *Complete Poems and Plays, 1909-1950*. Harcourt.

93 GEORGE ORWELL *Animal Farm*. London: Secker & Warburg, 1945.
h. Secker & Warburg. p. Penguin.
Down and Out in Paris and London, 1933.
h. Secker & Warburg. p. Penguin.
The Road to Wigan Pier, 1937.
h. Secker & Warburg. p. Penguin.
Homage to Catalonia, 1938.
h. Secker & Warburg. p. Penguin.

American editions
Animal Farm.
h. Harcourt.
p. introd. C. M. Woodhouse. New American Library: Signet Classics.
Down and Out in Paris and London.
h. Harcourt.
p. Berkley.
The Road to Wigan Pier.
h. Harcourt.
p. Berkley.

Homage to Catalonia.
h. Harcourt.
p. Boston: Beacon Pr.

94 ALBERT CAMUS *L'Étranger*. Paris: Gallimard, 1942.
f. Le livre de poche, 406; London: Methuen.
h. = *The Outsider*; trans. Stuart Gilbert; new edn. Hamish Hamilton, 1957.
p. as above. Penguin.
Included in *The Collected Fiction*, Hamish Hamilton.
Le mythe de Sisyphe, 1942.
f. Gallimard.
h. = *The Myth of Sisyphus*; trans. J. O'Brien. Hamish Hamilton.
Caligula, 1944.
f. Le livre de poche. [late 1965.]
h. = *Caligula & Cross Purpose*; trans. Stuart Gilbert. Hamish Hamilton.
Jean-Paul Sartre, *L'Être et le Néant*, 1943.
f. Gallimard.
h. = *Being and Nothingness*; trans. Hazel E. Barnes. Methuen.

American editions
L'Étranger.
h. = *L'Étranger*. (f.). Pantheon.
h., p. = *The Stranger*; trans. Stuart Gilbert. Knopf; Knopf: Vintage.
p. *L'Étranger*. (f.) eds. Germain Bree & Carlos Lynes, Jr. Appleton.
Le Myth de Sisyphe.
h., p. = *The Myth of Sisyphus and Other Essays*; trans. Justin O'Brien. Knopf; Knopf: Vintage.
Caligula
h., p. = *Caligula and Three Other Plays* (*The Misunderstanding; State of Siege; The Just Assassins*); trans. Stuart Gilbert. Knopf; Knopf: Vintage.
Jean-Paul Sartre, *L'Etre et le Néant.*
h. (selections) In: *The Philosophy of Jean-Paul Sartre*; ed. Robert Denoon Cumming. Random House.

95 ALBERT CAMUS *La Peste*. Paris: Gallimard, 1947.
f. Le livre de poche, 132; London: Methuen.
h. = *The Plague*; trans. Stuart Gilbert; new edn. Hamish Hamilton.
p. as above. Penguin.
Ernest Hemingway, *The Sun also Rises*.
See 49, 50.
For Whom the Bell Tolls, 1940.
h. Cape.
p. Penguin.

American editions

La Peste.
h. = *The Plague*; trans. Stuart Gilbert. Knopf.
h., p. = *The Plague*. Modern Library; Modern Library College Editions.
L'Étranger.
See 94.
Le Myth de Sisyphe.
See 94.
Ernest Hemingway, *The Sun Also Rises*.
See 49, 50.
For Whom the Bell Tolls.
h., p. Scribner; Scribner: Scribner Library.
p. selections in *The Hemingway Reader*; ed. Charles Poore. Scribner: Scribner Library.
André Malraux, *La Condition Humaine*.
See 77.

96 DYLAN THOMAS *Deaths and Entrances*. London: Dent, 1946.
h. Dent.
New Poems, 1943.
In Country Sleep, 1952.
See 78.

American editions

See 78.

97 JOHN BETJEMAN *Selected Poems*. London: Murray, 1948.
Mount Zion, 1931.

h. *Collected Poems*; compiled by the Earl of Birkenhead. Murray, 1958.
p. as above; 2nd edn. Murray, 1962.
A Few Late Chrysanthemums, 1949.
h. Murray.
Also *Collected Poems* as h, p. above.

American edition
h. *Collected Poems*. Houghton.

98 EZRA POUND *Pisan Cantos*. New York: New Directions, 1948. London: Faber, 1949.
h. *The Cantos*; new collected edn. Faber, 1964.

American editions
See 35, 66.

99 GEORGE ORWELL *Nineteen Eighty-four*. London: Secker & Warburg, 1949.
h. Secker & Warburg. p. Penguin.
Inside the Whale, 1940.
Critical Essays, 1946.
h, p. *Collected Essays*. Secker & Warburg.

American editions
Nineteen Eighty-four.
h. Harcourt.
p. = *1984*; afterword Erich Fromm. New American Library: Signet Classics.
p. *Nineteen Eighty-four: Text, Sources, Criticism*; ed. Irving Howe. Harcourt.
Inside the Whale.
Critical Essays.
p. *A Collection of Essays*. Doubleday: Anchor.
p. *The Orwell Reader: Fiction, Essays, and Reportage*. Harvest.

100 WILLIAM CARLOS WILLIAMS *Paterson 1, 2, 3, 4*. New York: New Directions, 1946-51.

h. *Paterson: Books 1-5*. MacGibbon & Kee.
p. *Paterson*, *1*, *2*, *3*, *4*, *5*. New York: New Directions.

American edition

h., p. *Paterson*, *1-5*. New Directions.